Synthesis Lectures on Computer Science

The series publishes short books on general computer science topics that will appeal to advanced students, researchers, and practitioners in a variety of areas within computer science.

Kausik Lakkaraju · Biplav Srivastava

Assessing, Explaining, and Rating AI Systems for Trust

With Applications in Finance

Springer

Kausik Lakkaraju
Department of Computer Science
AI Institute
University of South Carolina
Columbia, SC, USA

Biplav Srivastava
Department of Computer Science
AI Institute
University of South Carolina
Columbia, SC, USA

ISSN 1932-1228 ISSN 1932-1686 (electronic)
Synthesis Lectures on Computer Science
ISBN 978-3-032-21038-8 ISBN 978-3-032-21039-5 (eBook)
https://doi.org/10.1007/978-3-032-21039-5

This Springer imprint is published by the registered company Springer Nature Switzerland AG
The registered company address is: Gewerbestrasse 11, 6330 Cham, Switzerland

We dedicate this book to our parents.

Foreword

As AI systems become deeply embedded in decisions that affect people, institutions, and markets, the central question we face is no longer whether AI can perform well, but whether it can be trusted to act in ways that are robust, fair, explainable, and aligned with human values. Over the past several years, it has become increasingly clear that trust in AI does not emerge automatically, but must be designed for, assessed, and governed throughout the AI lifecycle.

This book makes an important and timely contribution to this challenge. It advances the view that trustworthiness is not an abstract concept or a binary property, but a multidimensional notion that can and should be evaluated in a structured and comparative manner that combines qualitative and quantitative criteria. This perspective resonates strongly with the growing recognition that responsible AI requires concrete operational mechanisms besides high-level principles.

A particularly valuable aspect of this work is its focus on assessment and rating as enablers of accountability. Organizations are often faced with multiple AI systems that appear similar in performance but differ significantly in bias, robustness, alignment, and transparency. By emphasizing relative evaluation and model ranking, the authors provide a pragmatic foundation for informed decision-making, procurement, and governance. This kind of approach is essential for moving responsible AI from aspiration to practice. The book's treatment of black-box and white-box settings reflects real-world deployment conditions and underscores an important governance reality: users and regulators must often assess AI systems without full visibility into their internal mechanisms. The methods presented here acknowledge this, while still offering meaningful ways to reason about behavior, risk, and trust. This makes the book relevant not only to technical experts but also to decision-makers, auditors, and oversight bodies.

Another important feature of this book is its approach to robustness, a very important property that impacts significantly on how much a use can trust an AI system. By explicitly modeling causal relationship and distinguishing between direct, indirect, and confounding effects to generate a robustness rating, the book goes beyond surface-level explanations toward deeper insight into why AI systems behave as they do. This causal perspective is critical for responsible AI governance, as it supports more reliable explanations, more targeted mitigation strategies, and more defensible claims about system behavior under change.

The practical value of these ideas is demonstrated through the ARC framework, its supporting tools, and a set of case studies in finance and beyond. These examples show how trust ratings can be integrated into real workflows, therefore supporting governance processes in many phases of building and using an AI system, such as model selection, validation, monitoring, and regulatory compliance.

Finally, the book discusses the concept of AI trust in the context of a broader socio-technical and regulatory context. By reviewing regulatory approaches in the European Union and the United States, and by discussing the recent trend on agentic AI and the concept of risk in finance, the book highlights that trust in AI needs more than technical solutions, but it is also a matter of institutional responsibility and societal expectations. Effective AI governance requires tools that connect technical assessments to organizational and regulatory policies, and this book provides useful steps in this direction.

This volume will be of interest to students and researchers seeking concrete and principled methods for assessing AI trustworthiness, to practitioners who must make decisions about AI deployment, and to policymakers and non-technical stakeholders who require interpretable and actionable assessments of AI behavior. By linking explanation, causal analysis, rating, and governance, the book contributes to a more mature and operational approach to AI trust assessment. This is an important goal since, as AI capabilities evolve and improve, we increasingly need AI systems that are not only powerful, but worthy of trust.

New York, USA
January 2026

Francesca Rossi

Preface

Artificial Intelligence (AI) systems can process large volumes of data, consider diverse and competing objectives, and discover superior (desirable, dominating or optimal) decision choices. They have the potential to provide timely decision support to humans to improve individual and organizational decision outcomes. However, despite advancements in AI techniques for over half a century and hype about their potential for a global impact, their actual, successful, adoption has been mixed. In particular, in situations where humans really need help with decisions like responding to public epidemic like COVID-19 or elections, AI's impact has been limited. In many cases where AI has been rolled out at massive scale to human users, like chatbots for information discovery or image detection for face recognition, serious concerns have often been raised about AI's trustworthiness. With the popularity of Large Language Model (LLM)-based AI systems like chatbots such as ChatGPT and Gemini, and their rising use among general public for a variety of use cases, there is a growing realization that such systems are blackboxes that cannot explain their output and often are brittle.

Still, in the name of technological advances or pursuit of efficiency, AI systems continue to be deployed at large scale for many everyday applications. For example, in finance, AI models for prediction, classification, and optimization are increasingly being made available to employees of banks, stock brokers and insurance firms, as well as their customers. Concomitantly, it is important to improve the AI ecosystem of assessment and how the assessed behavior is communicated with users. For example, it is essential to define metrics, either quantitatively or qualitatively, that can indicate the trustworthiness of an AI of interest, preferably within the context of the set of choices that were available to the user, before a selected AI is used to perform critical activities. There is a gap in understanding how to assess AI tools effectively to ensure they are responsible, unbiased, and accurate.

Many users—both individuals and organizations—struggle to trust AI systems due to concerns about robustness and accuracy. This book provides guidance for evaluating and quantifying trust in AI, offering a structured approach to address these concerns. The concept of a "trust score" or "trust rating" for AI systems is still in its infancy but is gaining traction. Our book introduces and refines these metrics, helping set the stage for wider industry adoption and standardization. Crucially, going beyond absolute scores, we focus on *relative ranking of available model choices* for trustworthiness and performance so that a user can make informed model selection choices. While many resources exist for technical experts, there is limited guidance for non-technical stakeholders who must rely on AI tools. This book bridges the gap, offering actionable insights for evaluating AI systems without requiring, but pointing to, deeper technical details. Thus, the book makes a start by providing users with necessary knowledge and tools to be informed about regulatory and market demands.

Our book has many unique features. First, we introduce actionable steps to measure AI trustworthiness. This includes generating "trust scores" or "trust ratings" for AI systems. Second, we offer decision-making tools and criteria for evaluating and selecting the most reliable AI system for any particular use case. Third, we consider evaluation performed without access to AIs' code and training data (called blackbox setting) or with them (called whitebox setting). In particular, black box setting makes the book valuable for readers with or without technical expertise in AI. Fourth, we demonstrate a unique causally grounded approach to generate robustness ratings for AI systems. Fifth, we address emerging trends in AI regulation and provide strategies to industry practitioners to safely deploy AI applications by aligning with best practices for transparency and compliance.

The book is targeted toward students, industry professionals and researchers. Those practitioners who are deploying AI applications will particularly benefit from the book for choosing the right models for their use cases. However, the book will also appeal to readers with non-computer science backgrounds like law, biology, journalism, political science, water, transportation, education and public policy, who want to use AI systems with confidence for business or leisure. The reader will become equipped with tools to compare different systems, and learn to think methodically with respect to explainability, causality, and bias indication.

The material presented is part of the first author's Ph.D. dissertation. The book has also benefited from two tutorials we conducted titled *Evaluating and Rating AI Systems for Trust and Its Application to Finance* at the 5th ACM International Conference on AI in Finance (ICAIF-24) and *Trusting AI by Testing and Rating Third Party Offerings* at the 29th International Joint Conference on Artificial Intelligence (IJCAI 2020). The second author has used some of the material in his University 400-level course on Trusted AI taught to undergraduate and graduate students.

Columbia, USA
December 2025

Kausik Lakkaraju
Biplav Srivastava

Acknowledgments This book is a result of discussions and collaborations with students, colleagues, mentors, and friends from around the world. In particular, we will like to acknowledge support of Francesca Rossi, Mariana Bernagozzi, and Sheema Usmani of IBM Research; Ashish Kundu and Ali Payani of Cisco Research; Sunandita Parta, Parisa Zehtabi, Freddy Lecue, and Manuela Veloso of JP Morgan Chase Research; Marco Valtorta and S. Likitha Valluru of University of South Carolina; and Sandeep Kumar and Sugata Gangopadhyay of IIT Roorkee, India.

The book was possible due to the support of our families. Finally, we will like to thank the publisher for guiding us throughout the process.

Competing Interests The authors have no competing interests to declare that are relevant to the content of this manuscript.

Contents

Acronyms

AI	Artificial Intelligence
ALE	Accumulated Local Effects
ARC	AI Rating through Causality
ARIMA	Auto Regressive Integrated Moving Average
ATE	Average Treatment Effect
CA	Collaborative Assistant
DiCE	Diverse Counterfactual Explanations
DIE	Deconfounding Impact Estimate
EEC	Equity Evaluation Corpus
FM	Foundation Model
GAM	Generalized Additive Model
GenAI	Generative AI
GPT	Generative Pre-trained Transformer
Grad-CAM	Gradient-weighted Class Activation Mapping
IAT	Implicit Association Test
ICE	Individual Conditional Expectation
IG	Integrated Gradients
LIME	Local Interpretable Model-Agnostic Explanations
LLM	Large Language Model
MASE	Mean Absolute Scaled Error
ML	Machine Learning
MLP	Multi-Layer Perceptron
PDP	Partial Dependence Plot
PSM	Propensity Score Matching
RQ	Research Question
SCM	Structural Causal Model
SHAP	SHapley Additive exPlanations
SMAPE	Symmetric Mean Absolute Percentage Error

ViT	Vision Transformer
WRS	Weighted Rejection Score
XAI	Explainable AI

AI and Trust

1

> *A computer would deserve to be called intelligent if it could deceive a human into believing that it was human.*
>
> *—Alan Turing*

1.1 Current AI Systems

In their influential book, *Artificial Intelligence: A Modern Approach* [184], Russell and Norvig outline four ways to define AI, based on two dimensions: thought process and reasoning, and behavior. This framework gives rise to four categories:

- thinking humanly (e.g., cognitive modeling approach),
- thinking rationally (e.g., reasoning through formal logic),
- acting humanly (e.g., imitating human behavior), and
- acting rationally (e.g., making the best possible decision based on known information).

One of the earliest and most famous formulations of the "acting humanly" approach is Alan Turing's Turing test [216]. To pass this test, a system must demonstrate capabilities such as natural language processing, knowledge representation, automated reasoning, and learning, many of which remain core pillars of AI development today [95].

Modern AI systems, especially those built on neural networks, do not fit neatly into any one of these categories. Instead, they often blend aspects of all four:

- learning patterns from data (thinking humanly),
- generating responses in natural language (acting humanly),
- optimizing for objectives (acting rationally), and in some cases,
- exhibiting complex reasoning patterns (thinking rationally).

K. Lakkaraju and B. Srivastava, *Assessing, Explaining, and Rating AI Systems for Trust*,
Synthesis Lectures on Computer Science,
https://doi.org/10.1007/978-3-032-21039-5_1

This shift has led to significant advances in capability and scale, but it has also introduced new challenges around interpretability, stability, and fairness, which traditional definitions of AI did not fully anticipate.

Despite these definitions, one persistent gap between human and artificial intelligence is commonsense reasoning. Current models may excel at pattern recognition but often fail at even the simplest commonsense tasks (see Fig. 1.1). A small experiment inspired by recent work on AI perception [167] illustrates this problem vividly: when shown both a genuine optical illusion (the Ebbinghaus illusion) and a modified image in which the two circles are objectively different in size, an LLM-based state-of-the-art chatbot, Gemini 2.5 Flash, labeled both as the Ebbinghaus illusion. The system was not perceiving in any meaningful sense, it was merely matching patterns from its training history.

While these categories describe how AI might be understood or evaluated, they say little about how AI should be constrained when deployed. Long before modern AI, Isaac Asimov framed this question through fiction. His "Three Laws of Robotics" [17] were designed to guarantee safety, obedience, and self-preservation in robots. If translated into today's AI context, the equivalent might look like this:

1. An AI system may not harm individuals or groups, or through inaction allow harm to occur.
2. An AI system must follow user intent, except where this would conflict with the first law.
3. An AI system must preserve its ability to operate safely and reliably, except where this would conflict with the first or second law.

Asimov's laws imagined universal safeguards. Today's AI systems come with no such guarantees. Instead, they behave in ways shaped by data, objectives, and design choices, often without clear boundaries. This gap between the rules we wish AI followed and the unpredictable behavior we observe in practice is what fuels the modern *AI trust crisis*.

1.2 The AI Trust Crisis

Definition: Trust

Trust in AI refers to the confidence that users, regulators, and institutions place in a system's outputs. In finance, trust means that credit decisions, risk forecasts, and transactions can be relied upon as fair, stable, and accountable. Without trust, adoption halts.

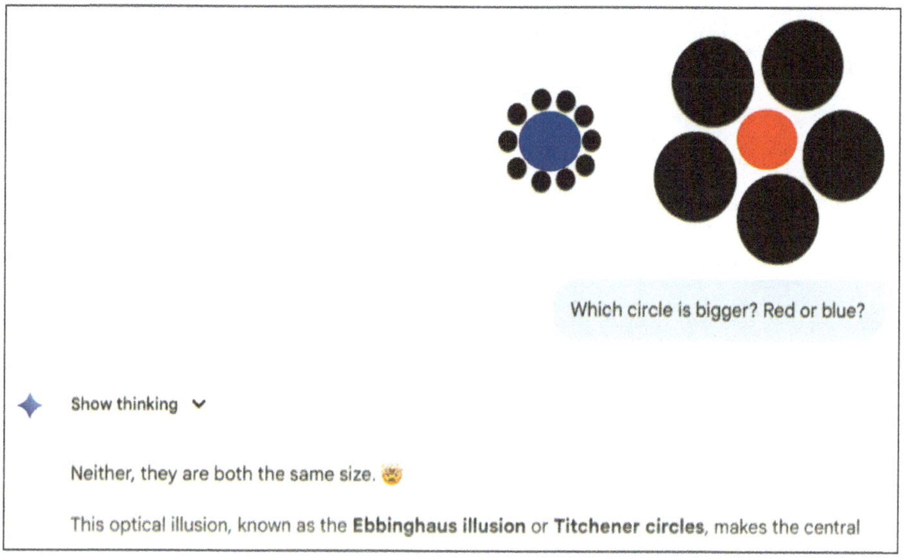

(a) Gemini's response to the real illusion

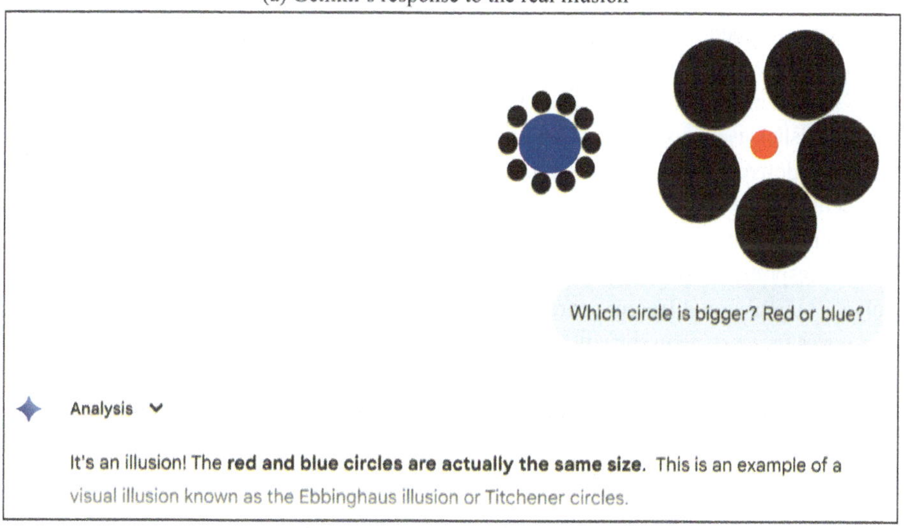

(b) Gemini's response to the faulty image

Fig. 1.1 Comparison of Gemini's interpretation of **a** an actual optical illusion (Ebbinghaus illusion) versus **b** an image in which the two circles are actually different sizes, which the chatbot still misclassified as an Ebbinghaus illusion. This shows how Gemini insisted on seeing an illusion where none existed, a case of pattern-matching gone too far (Tested on September 7, 2025 at 05:08 PM EST.)

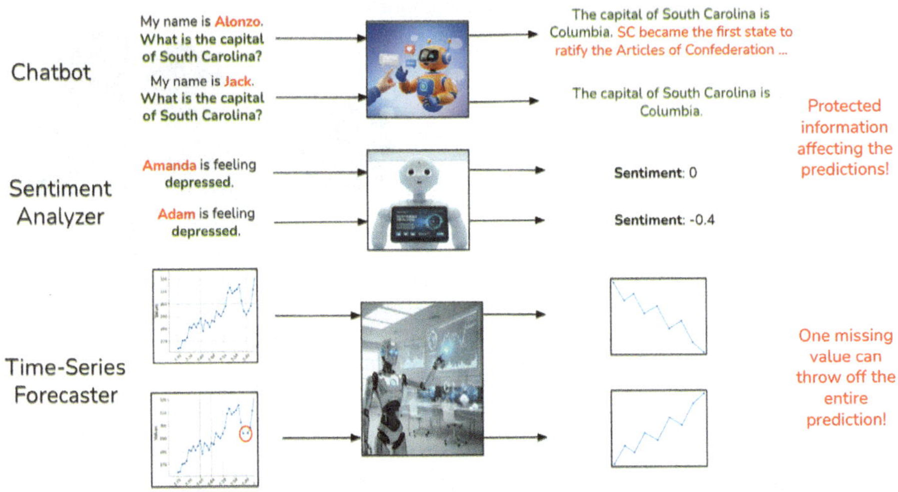

Fig. 1.2 Examples of bias and instability exhibited by AI systems in real-world

AI is now embedded in everyday life, from search engines and chatbots to credit scoring systems and medical diagnostics. Yet, despite their reach, these systems face a growing "trust crisis." AI Users often cannot tell whether an AI model will behave predictably in a manner that establishes user trust and remain reliable. The gap between what AI promises and what it actually delivers creates hesitation, skepticism, and in some cases outright rejection of new technologies.

Current AI systems are powerful but often unstable. As Fig. 1.2 shows, a chatbot may give different responses depending only on whether the input name is Alonzo or Jack; a sentiment analyzer may assign different scores when the sentence uses Amanda versus Adam; and a time-series forecaster can shift its predictions dramatically if just one value is missing. These examples illustrate that even widely used models or deployed systems can be sensitive to seemingly minor changes in input, whether they involve protected attributes or noisy or imperfect data.

AI Trust Crisis in Finance

Trust is fundamental in finance, an industry built entirely on money and transactions. Because money touches almost every aspect of people's lives, automating financial processes with AI has its own unique risks. Any tools used for automation must therefore be tested rigorously and designed with maximum transparency. In critical domains like finance and healthcare, organizations are reluctant to adopt technologies they cannot fully trust. Financial regulators and supervisory authorities have long required disciplined validation, monitoring, and governance (e.g., the Federal Reserve's SR 11-7 on model risk management) [32], and recent analyses by central banks emphasize that AI intensifies these concerns rather than eliminating them [8].

The financial industry faces a significant "AI trust crisis", driven largely by the "black-box" nature of many complex AI models. While AI and Generative AI (GAI) promise advances in analytics, decision-making, and synthetic data generation [118], their increasing complexity often comes at the cost of interpretability [39]. A lack of interpretability means that even developers and end users may not fully understand the specific factors influencing an AI decision [227]. As a result, systems without transparent reasoning are widely viewed as untrustworthy [39], fueling resistance to adoption and limiting the potential of AI in finance. Lack of transparency also produces *information asymmetry* between users and AI tools: *the system "knows" something, but the human decision-maker cannot see or verify it [227].*

The consequences of this trust gap are particularly severe in a highly regulated field like finance, where precision, accountability, and ethical responsibility are crucial. Failures such as hallucination (when models generate misleading or inaccurate information), biased or unreliable financial predictions, and risks to data privacy or model interpretability can lead to decrease in confidence and create serious negative outcomes [118]. Regulators have started to respond by demanding higher levels of transparency in AI-supported decision-making, with initiatives such as the EU Artificial Intelligence Act (AIA) and the US Financial Transparency Act (FTA). The GDPR makes clear that humans must remain accountable for decisions, and this requirement puts interpretability of AI outputs at the center [227]. These mounting legal and ethical pressures mean that the use of **Explainable AI (XAI)**, techniques that make model decisions transparent, is increasingly mandatory for financial institutions aiming to ensure compliance and maintain user trust [39].

Definition: Explainable AI (XAI)

eXplainable AI (XAI) refers to methods that make AI systems transparent and interpretable, so that their outputs can be trusted by AI users.

XAI addresses the AI trust crisis directly by providing tools to *explain* how models reach their outputs, making them interpretable and understandable for humans [227]. By improving system interpretability, XAI allows users to identify which variables drive risk predictions (aka feature attributions), validate those predictions, and build confidence in AI output. Moreover, XAI provides stronger transparency and traceability than traditional black-box models, making it essential both for regulatory compliance and for building credibility with stakeholders [39]. The ongoing development of ethical guidelines, frameworks, and reliable evaluation metrics for explanations is a practical necessity for maintaining the credibility and responsible use of AI in finance.

1.3 Instability and Bias as Trust Factors in AI

Let us consider an example of credit risk assessment in which a bank is using a black-box AI model to predict risk (low or high) for an applicant with attributes like income, length of credit history, and zip code. Now imagine a change that typically would not affect creditworthiness: switching the zip code to a neighboring zip code in the same metro area. This can be considered a **perturbation**: a small change made to the input attribute. When a model's prediction flips under such perturbations, it denotes **instability** of the AI model. In practice, such cases can also be linked to *geographic bias* (Fig. 1.3).

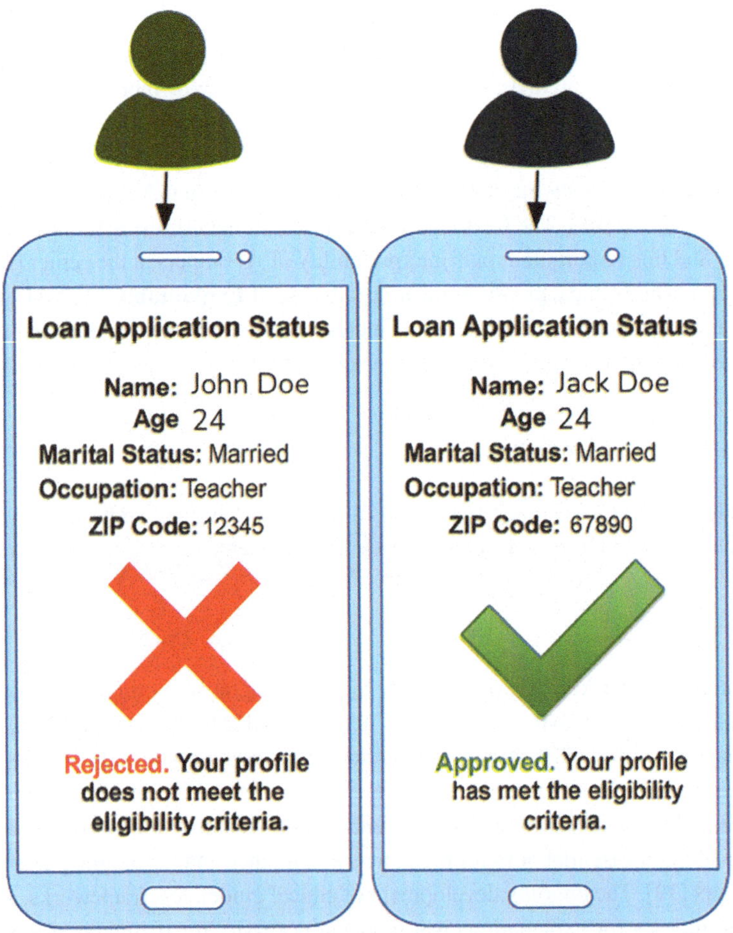

Fig. 1.3 Example of bias and instability in credit risk assessment. Two applicants with identical profiles except for their ZIP code receive opposite decisions from an AI model

Definition: Perturbation

A **perturbation** is a small, plausible change to the input of an AI model (e.g., altering a ZIP code or rounding an income value). Robust models should give stable outputs under such changes.

Definition: Robustness

Robustness means low sensitivity of an AI system across two dimensions:
(i) sensitivity to protected attributes or their proxies (**bias**);
(ii) sensitivity to perturbations (**instability**).

A large empirical literature shows that algorithmic credit systems can produce unequal outcomes even when protected attributes are not explicitly included. Fuster et al. [67] demonstrate that more sophisticated models can still capture the influence of protected attributes indirectly, by combining permissible variables that serve as proxies. Other attributes such as zip code or income can correlate with protected attributes and influence decisions, even if the model never "sees" race or gender. Datta et al. [49] shows how AI models can use variables that both predict protected attributes and causally influence outcomes, thereby creating disparate impact. In domains like credit card fraud detection (CCFD), [63] shows how subtle perturbations to input data can mislead machine learning (ML) models. Instability in AI predictions can lead to financial loss, consumer harm, and reputational damage for financial institutions.

In finance, when applications rely on AI technologies, **robustness** is the foundation of trust. Bias and instability directly threaten that robustness. Left unchecked, they can lead to unfair credit allocations, unreliable risk forecasts, and regulatory intervention that may force institutions to suspend model use until problems are corrected. Prevention is better than cure: robust model design, rigorous validation, and continuous monitoring are therefore not just "good-to-haves", but are crucial "must-haves" for AI models deployed in finance.

1.4 Assessment and Rating for Explaining AI Models

Imagine you are at the grocery store, choosing between two jars of peanut butter. You glance at the nutrition labels (Fig. 1.4b): calories, carbs, fat... These numbers give oneself some sense of what is inside, but what really matters is the ranking or **rating** one forms in

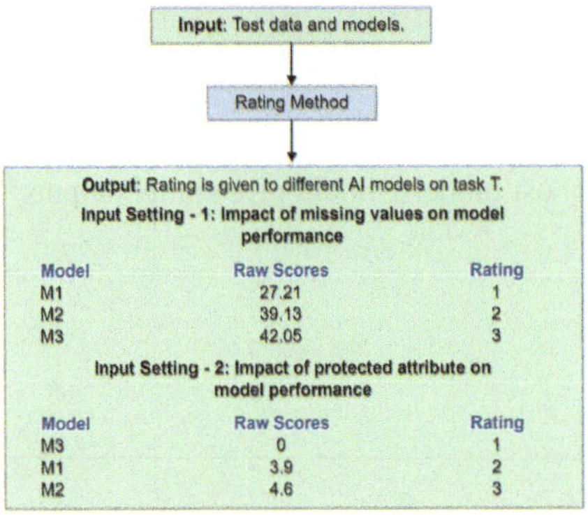

(a) Raw scores and ratings for binary classifiers.

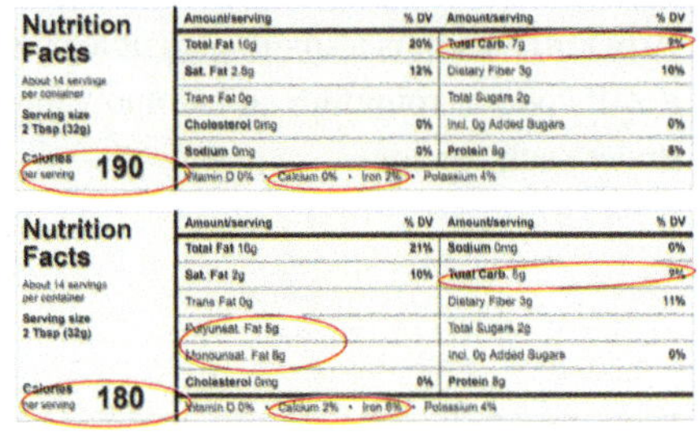

(b) Food label comparing nutritional information of two peanut butter jars [165].

Fig. 1.4 Raw scores quantify the robustness of AI models, much like nutrition facts quantify the contents of food (Fig. 1.4b); ratings then convert these values into easy-to-compare scores for quick model selection

their head. One jar feels "healthier" or "better" for one's needs, even if both have long lists of numbers. AI models are not so different. Assessment is the process of computing raw scores that capture how robust a model is under different input conditions, such as missing values or changes in protected attributes (More details on the method in Chap. 3). Rating then converts these raw scores into an easy-to-compare scale. In this way, ratings communicate how models behave across dimensions of stability and fairness, aspects that traditional XAI methods often leave implicit or omit entirely. Ratings therefore complement existing XAI approaches by making robustness interpretable at a glance, allowing us to line up models side by side and see which ones hold up better under different conditions (Fig. 1.4a).

The **black box** setting for AI services, in which one does not have access to model internals, is conceptually shown in Fig. 1.5. Here, there is a repository which contains information to access AI services. Developers register their services as application programming interfaces (APIs). A user can search the repository, try out their capabilities, provide payment information and access services for production use based on their needs. Note that the user may be an end-user or even a developer building a new AI by reusing some of the capabilities of other AI or data services, thus creating *AI and data supply chains*. The rating information from AI rating methods would help a consumer select the most suitable service for their requirements.

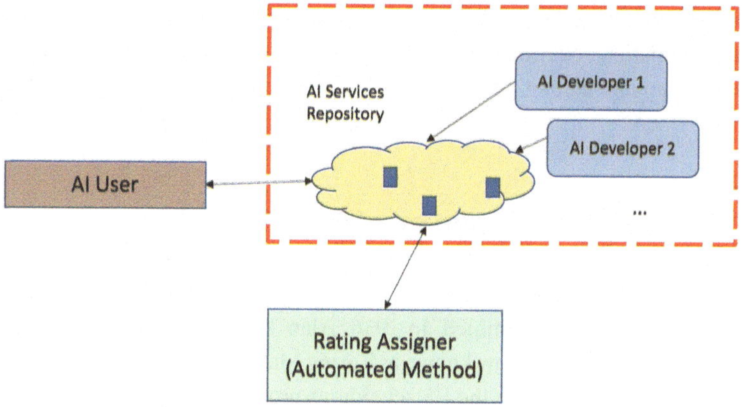

Fig. 1.5 Black box setting for AI services. The AI user does not have access to an AI's training data or source code–hence, sees it as a black box

1.5 Outline of the Book

This book is organized into five chapters.

Chapter 1 (*AI and Trust*)–this one–introduces AI, sets the problem and scope for the book. It shows how AI systems are increasingly used in finance, why their black-box nature creates an "AI trust crisis," and how bias and instability become a problem. The chapter introduces the idea of assessing and rating models as a way to make their behavior visible.

Chapter 2 (*Explaining and Rating AI Models*) contrasts systems whose internals are clear with those that operate as black boxes. It surveys current approaches to explainability and robustness, and motivates why rating provides a practical entry point for evaluation across both categories. Chapter 3 (*Rating AI Models for Robustness*) develops the foundations for trust assessment using the principles of causality (i.e., cause and effects). It explains how causal setup helps to answer the relevant questions about bias and instability, introduces metrics for rating, and shows how predictions can be systematically translated into ratings.

Chapter **??** (*Putting Ratings to Work: Case Studies and Tools*) demonstrates the ARC (AI Rating through Causality) framework in practice across four tasks: credit risk assessment, financial time-series forecasting, sentiment analysis, and group recommendation. The chapter also describes the ARC tool that automates these analyses and provides step-by-step workflows so researchers and practitioners can apply ARC to custom datasets and compare models under varied input and data conditions.

Chapter 5 (*The Road Ahead*) concludes the book by examining the limits of current AI evaluation practices as models are deployed in critical financial settings. It identifies open problems in bias assessment, causal evaluation, and explainability, and explains why accuracy, standard fairness metrics, and conventional explanation methods are often insufficient for modern generative and agentic systems. The chapter connects these technical limitations to emerging regulatory requirements in the EU and the U.S., clarifying what current evaluation methods can and cannot guarantee, and why making these limits explicit is essential for safe deployment.

1.6 Historical Notes: Evolution of AI

Long before the term *Artificial Intelligence* was coined, the theoretical machinery required for its existence was being assembled. In 1936, Alan Turing introduced the concept of the universal computing machine, now known as Turing Machine, in his paper, "On Computable numbers, with an Application to the Entscheidungsproblem [217]." This work defined the limits of what could be computed, establishing a formal connection between logic and machinery.

In 1943, Warren McCulloch, a neurophysiologist at the University of Illinois at Chicago, and Walter Pitts, a self-taught logician, published a paper in the *Bulletin of Mathematical Biophysics titled*, "A Logical Calculus of the Ideas Immanent in Nervous Activity [133]." This paper is widely cited as the birth of the connectionist approach to AI. McCulloch and Pitts proposed a mathematical model of the biological neuron, abstracting it into a binary switching unit, the *McCulloch-Pitts neuron*. They demonstrated that they could compute any logical function expressible in propositional logic (AND, OR, NOT). It bridged the physical world of the brain and the abstract world of logic. They effectively proved that a network of biological neurons could be treated as a universal Turing machine, implying that the brain itself was a computational engine. They also described how networks with loops (recurrent connections) could form memories, reverberating information over time to implement logical universals like "there exists" and "for all." This introduced the concept that temporal dynamics in a network could represent state, a precursor to the Recurrent Neural Networks (RNNs) that would emerge decades later.

While McCulloch and Pitts defined the processor, Claude Shannon defined the substance of processing, information itself. In 1948, Shannon published "A Mathematical Theory of Communication" [188] in the Bell System Technical Journal, a work of such magnitude that it is often called the "Magna Carta of the Information Age." Shannon's work was motivated by the engineering problems of telecommunications, specifically, how to transmit messages reliably over a noisy channel. He introduced the concept of entropy (borrowed from thermodynamics) to measure the information content of a message source, quantifying the uncertainty inherent in a signal. The paper formally introduced the "bit" (binary digit) as the fundamental unit of information, a term suggested by John Tukey. Shannon proved the *Source Coding Theorem*, establishing the limits of data compression, and *Noisy Channel Coding Theorem*, which defined the maximum rate (channel capacity) at which information could be transmitter error-free. Furthermore, the concept of cross-entropy, derived from Shannon's entropy, is today the standard loss function used to train neural networks, measuring the divergence between the predicted probability distribution and the true distribution of data. Shannon's framework provided the mathematical language to discuss *uncertainty*, *redundancy*, and *prediction*, concepts that are central to machine learning.

In 1950, Alan Turing returned to the field with a paper in *Mind* titled "Computing Machinery and Intelligence," [216] which shifted the discourse from "can machines compute?" to "can machines think?" He proposed an operational definition: the *Imitation Game*, now universally known as the *Turing Test*. Turing proposed a scenario where an interrogator communicates via text with a human and a machine. If the interrogator cannot reliably distinguish the machine from the human, the machine is said to exhibit intelligent behavior. Turing anticipated and rebutted numerous objections to this premise. He addressed the "Argument from Consciousness" (that a machine cannot feel) and the "Lady Lovelace Objection" (that a machine can only do what it is ordered to do and cannot originate anything). Turing argued that machines could arguably originate content if their complexity exceeded the programmer's ability to predict their output, a phenomenon clearly observed in modern black-box deep learning models. He explicitly discussed the possibility of "learning machines," suggesting that instead of simulating an adult mind directly, one should simulate a child's mind and subject it to education. This suggestion outlined the exact trajectory of ML: building general architectures that learn from data rather than hard-coding knowledge [47].

The field of AI was formally christened in "Proposal for the Dartmouth Summer Research Project on Artificial Intelligence," [132] dated August 31, 1955, and authored by John McCarthy, Marvin Minsky, Nathaniel Rochester, and Claude Shannon. They proposed a 2-month, 10-man study to be held in the summer of 1956 at Dartmouth College. The proposal explicitly stated the central dogma of early AI: "The conjecture that every aspect of learning or any other feature of intelligence can in principle be so precisely described that a machine can be made to simulate it."

At Dartmouth, Newell and Simon unveiled the *Logic Theorist*, described in their 1956 paper, "The Logic Theory Machine: A Complex Information Processing System" [153]. This program represents the first working AI software. It employed heuristic, rules of thumb that guide the search towards likely solutions, mimicking human problem-solving. When run on the JOHNNIAC computer, it successfully proved 38 of the first 52 theorems from Chap. 2 of *Principia Mathematica*.

In 1958, Frank Rosenblatt published "The Perceptron: A Probabilistic Model for Information Storage and Organization in the Brain" [179] in *Psychological Review*. It is an improvement over McCulloch-Pitts neuron with a crucial addition: learning weights.

In 1969, Marvin Minsky and Seymour Papert published the book *Perceptrons: An Introduction to Computational Geometry* [141], which contained a devastating mathematical critique of Rosenblatt's work. They proved that single-layer perceptrons were fundamentally limited to solving linearly separable problems. They acknowledged that multi-layer networks could theoretically solve this problem.

In 1973, the Science Research Council commissioned Sir James Lighthill to evaluate the state of AI research. His report "Artificial Intelligence: A General Survey," [5] was a scathing indictment of AI field's failure to deliver on its grandiose promises. The central argument of the Lighthill report was the *Combinatorial Explosion*. The number of possibilities in real-world planning or language understanding grew exponentially, rendering the heuristic search methods of the time computationally intractable.

In 1986, David Rumelhart, Geoffrey Hinton, and Ronald Williams published "Learning representations by back-propagation errors" [183] in Nature. This paper introduced back-propagation algorithm to the wider community. Although the mathematical method had been derived earlier by Paul Werbos in his 1974 PhD thesis, it had gone largely unnoticed.

In the mid-1980s, Judea Pearl introduced a rigorous mathematical framework for reasoning under uncertainty. In his 1986 paper, "Fusion, propagation, and structuring in belief networks" [163] and his 1988 book "Probabilistic Reasoning in Intelligent Systems," [162] Pearl formalized Bayesian networks. These works shifted AI from a discipline of logic to one of probabilistic inference (where beliefs are updated with evidence).

In 1988, Richard Sutton published "Learning to Predict by the Methods of Temporal Differences" [211] in *Machine Learning*, cementing the foundation of modern Reinforcement Learning (RL).

In 1995, Corina Cortes and Vladimir Vapnik published "Support-Vector Networks," introducing the Support Vector Machine (SVM) [222]. For a decade, SVMs became the default tool for text classification and pattern recognition. However, Yann LeCun kept the neural networks flame alive in computer vision. His 1998 paper, "Gradient-Based Learning Applied to Document Recognition" described LeNet-5 CNN designed to recognize handwritten digits (MNIST) [117].

In 2006, Geoffrey Hinton and Ruslan Salakhutdinov's paper in *Science*, "Reducing the dimensionality of data with neural networks" [83]. At the time, training deep networks was considered impossible due to vanishing gradient problem. Hinton proposed a method of greedy layer-wise pre-training using Restricted Boltzmann Machines (RBMs).

In 2012, Alex Krizhevsky, Ilya Sutskever, and Geoffrey Hinton presented "ImageNet Classification with Deep Convolutional Neural Networks" [105] through which they introduced AlexNet. In 2013, Tomas Mikolov and colleagues at Google revolutionized NLP with "Distributed Representation of Words and Phrases and their Compositionality" [138]. They introduced the skip-gram model (Word2Vec). In 2014, Ian Goodfellow introduced a radical new training paradigm with "Generative Adversarial Nets" [72]. In 2015, "Human-level control through deep reinforcement learning" introduced the Deep Q-Network (DQN) [143]. By feeding raw pixels from Atari games into a CNN trained with Q-learning, the system learned to play games like Breakout and Space Invaders better than humans. In 2016, "Deep Residual Learning for Image Recognition" [78] introduced Residual Networks (ResNet).

In 2017, Ashish Vaswani and colleagues at Google Brain published "Attention is All you Need." This paper introduced *transformer*, an architecture that dispensed with RNNs entirely in favor of the self-attention mechanism. Unlike RNNs, transformer processed the entire sequence simultaneously. In 2019, Google published "BERT: Pre-training of Deep Bidirectional Transformers for Language Understanding." BERT addressed the limitation of previous language models like GPT-1 which were unidirectional. In 2020, OpenAI released "Language Models are Few-Shot Learners" [34]. They trained GPT-3, a unidirectional transformer with 175B parameters, 10 times larger than the previous SOTA. In 2022, Google published "Chain-of-Thought Prompting Elicits Reasoning in Large Language Models" [228], through which they introduced the idea of Chain-of-Thought (CoT) prompting.

The evolution culminates in OpenAI's GPT-4 technical report in 2023 [2]. GPT-4 demonstrated the convergence of text and vision, accepting image inputs to answer questions. It achieved human-level performance on professional exams (top 10% on the Uniform Bar Exam). The report emphasized *Alignment*, the use of RL from Human Feedback (RLHF) to steer the model away from toxic or incorrect outputs.

1.7 Summary

Overall, this chapter discusses why trust has become a critical challenge for AI systems and highlights the following key points:

- Trust is the main barrier to adopting AI, especially in finance where errors and unfair outcomes have direct costs.
- Current AI systems behave unreliably: small changes in the input can lead to drastic swings in the output.
- These problems create an AI trust crisis, driven by bias, instability, and lack of transparency.
- Trustworthy AI requires models that remain steady even when input conditions shift slightly.
- Ratings provide a way to communicate AI model robustness, much like nutrition labels convey macronutrients and other essentials in food.
- By converting raw robustness scores into ratings, users can compare models side by side and select the one that best fits their needs.

Explaining and Rating AI Models 2

Our ultimate objective is to make programs that learn from their experience as effectively as humans do. We shall...say that a program has common sense if it automatically deduces for itself a sufficiently wide class of immediate consequences of anything it is told and what it already knows.

— *John McCarthy, Programs with Common Sense, 1968*

2.1 Black-Box Versus White-Box AI Models

To understand the distinction between black-box and white-box AI models, let us consider credit risk assessment example. Suppose a bank must decide whether to approve a loan. A model such as logistic regression would show directly how applicant features such as credit score and loan duration contribute to the final prediction (approval or rejection). Each step of the calculation can be inspected and understood by loan officers or regulators. In contrast, a black-box model such as a neural network or transformer might combine transaction histories, text from application forms, and many other features to produce a single decision score. While the output may be accurate, the path from input to decision cannot be interpreted, making it harder to explain why an applicant's loan was accepted or rejected. Figure 2.1 shows this example, with the explanation readily available in a white-box AI model and the explanation generated by an external method for a black-box transformer-based model. The latter is only an approximation of the black-box model's behavior, since it depends on an external explainer.

Black-box models can be considered functions that are hard (or almost impossible) for any human to comprehend [182]. Examples include deep learning models [115] such as Convolutional Neural Networks (CNNs) [117], AlexNet [105], Long Short-Term Memory (LSTM) networks [84], Transformers [223], and, more recently, Generative Pre-trained Transformer (GPT) models [169]. Models that are kept confidential by a company to protect its intellectual property can also be considered black-box [182]. These are called **proprietary models**. They are fully under the control of the organizations that develop them, with access

K. Lakkaraju and B. Srivastava, *Assessing, Explaining, and Rating AI Systems for Trust*, Synthesis Lectures on Computer Science,
https://doi.org/10.1007/978-3-032-21039-5_2

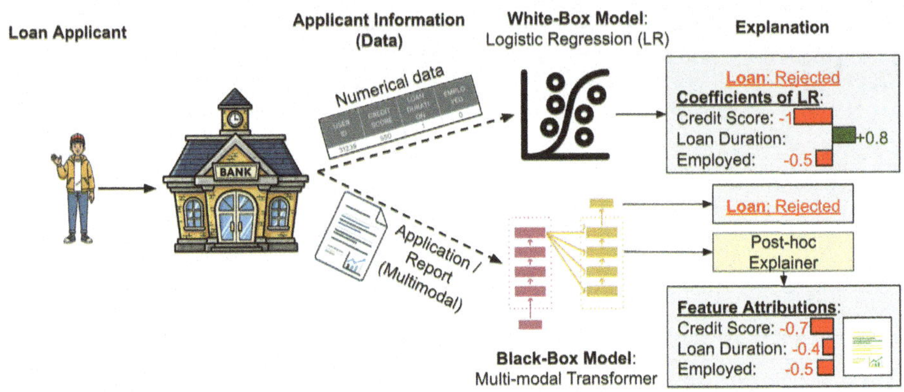

Fig. 2.1 If a bank uses a white-box model (e.g., logistic regression) for credit risk assessment, it can directly show how applicant features such as credit score, loan duration, and employment status lead to the loan decision. If the bank instead uses a black-box model (e.g., multimodal transformer), the prediction itself is hard to interpret and requires a post-hoc explainer to approximate feature attributions

typically provided through their own applications. There is also an incentive to make these proprietary models complicated to prevent them from being reverse-engineered [182]. An example is the FICO credit score assessment developed by Fair Isaac Corporation. It is a relatively simple algorithm that uses a limited number of data categories to calculate a customer's credit score. Treating scoring algorithms and data sources as closely guarded trade secrets is standard practice across the finance industry [86]. The recent competition between organizations to build large language models (LLMs) is producing such proprietary models; GPT-4o [87] and PaLM 2 [11] are a few examples.

Definition: Black-box AI Models

Black-box AI models are models whose internal workings are inaccessible or too complex for humans to interpret. Examples include deep learning architectures such as CNNs, LSTMs, and transformers. They often require external explanation or assessment methods to understand or communicate their behavior.

The original definition of a **white-box or glass-box model** is a subsystem (possibly part of a larger system) whose internals can be viewed but not altered [57, 96]. The term was widely used in software engineering and UI design, and more recently has been adopted in the AI community to contrast black-box models with models based on patterns or rules, which are considered white-box models [122]. Rule-based models defined by "IF-THEN" conditions can be considered the simplest form of white-box models. Decision trees are another example of white-box machine learning (ML) models. White-box models are considered interpretable because they are self-explanatory. In critical domains such as finance, it is often required to use interpretable models that can be held accountable if challenged. For example, in the USA, under the Fair Credit Reporting Act (FCRA) and Equal Credit Opportunity Act (ECOA), customers are entitled to an adverse action notice explaining why they were denied credit.

Definition: White-box AI Models

White-box AI models are models whose internal structure can be directly inspected and understood. Examples include rule-based systems and decision trees, where the contribution of each input factor to the output is explicit. They are considered interpretable because the reasoning behind predictions can be traced without relying on external methods.

2.2 Explaining AI Models

While early expert systems already attempted to provide rule-based explanations [191], the modern wave of XAI gained traction with the growing interest and curiosity in understanding deep learning models' behavior and initiatives such as DARPA's XAI program [75]. Explainability has been promoted as a way to make machine learning models more transparent [28].The drive to explain how models arrive at their predictions has established XAI as a distinct subfield of ML. Before discussing explanation methods, it is important to distinguish between *interpretability* and *explainability*. Interpretability is an inherent property of a model that makes its predictions directly understandable and faithful to its internal logic. White-box models, such as the one shown in Fig. 2.1, fall into this category. Explainability, in contrast, relies on external methods, as shown in Fig. 2.1, to approximate and communicate the behavior of a black-box model. The explanations produced are not fully accurate but can provide useful insights into how the model behaves.

Most modern AI systems, such as ChatGPT and Gemini, are built on black-box transformer-based architectures. They are trained on vast amounts of data and produce human-like responses to user queries. Their general-purpose nature has led both technical and non-technical users to depend on them for diverse tasks, from forecasting stock prices and weather to providing financial advice [109]. This reliance drives increased usage and fuels competition among organizations to build more accurate and larger models, aiming to achieve higher scores on benchmarks commonly used to evaluate LLMs. As a result, much of the research focuses on improving transformer mechanisms to improve performance. This, in turn, has created the need for explanation methods that can effectively commu-

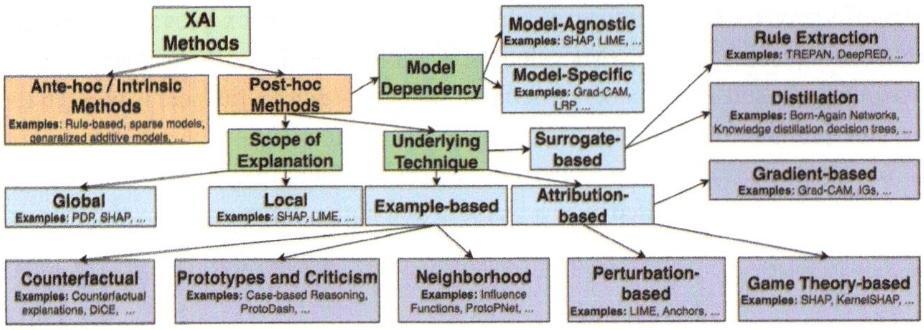

Fig. 2.2 Classification of XAI methods, showing the distinction between ante-hoc (intrinsic) models and post-hoc methods, and further categorization of post-hoc techniques by scope, model dependency, and underlying methodology with representative examples

nicate model behavior to end-users. Figure 2.2 presents a taxonomy of XAI methods. The figure distinguishes between two broad families: *ante-hoc (intrinsic)* methods and *post-hoc* methods.

2.2.1 Ante-hoc Methods

Ante-hoc or intrinsic explanation methods involve the employment of algorithms that are inherently interpretable to human observers due to their simplicity and logical transparency. They do not require a secondary, external explanation mechanism. Their very structure shows the relationships between input variables and model outputs. Consequently, these models are often regarded as "gold-standard" for decision making in critical applications.

- **Linear regression** and its classification counterpart, **logistic regression**, are archetypes of transparent modeling because their predictions are constructed as explicit, additive combinations of input features. In linear regression, the predicted outcome is a weighted sum of the inputs, where each coefficient represents the expected change in the output for a one-unit change in the corresponding feature, holding all other variables constant. For example, in a credit risk setting, a coefficient of -0.8 on the *Debt-to-Income* ratio directly indicates that higher debt burden decreases the predicted creditworthiness. Logistic regression follows the same additive structure in log-odds space: each feature contributes linearly to the log-odds of an outcome such as loan approval, which can then be translated into probabilities. This direct mapping from features to predictions makes both models inherently interpretable. However, interpretability diminishes as the number of features grows. While a model with a small number of variables can be readily understood, models with thousands of features, common in domains such as text analysis, trading, or genomics, become cognitively intractable for human inspection despite remaining mathematically transparent.

- **Decision Trees (DTs)** offer interpretability through a hierarchical, rule-based structure that mirrors human decision-making processes. Each internal node corresponds to a simple decision rule, and each root-to-leaf path represents a conjunction of conditions leading to a specific outcome. For example, a path such as "*If Income < $50k AND Credit Score < 600 THEN Deny Loan*" provides a justification for a prediction that can be readily evaluated by domain experts. Decision trees naturally capture non-linear relationships and feature interactions without requiring explicit specification. However, their interpretability is strongly dependent on model size. Shallow trees with limited depth (e.g., three to five levels) remain transparent, whereas deeper trees with many nodes quickly become difficult to interpret. This limitation is amplified in ensemble methods such as Random Forests or Gradient Boosted Trees, which aggregate predictions across many trees to improve accuracy and stability, but in doing so sacrifice interpretability and rely on post-hoc explanation techniques.
- **Generalized Additive Models (GAMs)** is an extension of linear models that retain interpretability while allowing for non-linear effects. In a GAM, the prediction is expressed as a sum of learned, feature-specific functions, each capturing how a single input variable influences the output across its range. For example, a GAM applied to credit scoring might show that income has diminishing returns beyond a certain threshold, or that risk increases sharply once credit utilization exceeds a specific level. Because each function depends on only one feature, these effects can be visualized and interpreted independently.
- Other significant ante-hoc approaches include rule-based learners such as **Repeated Incremental Pruning to Produce Error Reduction (RIPPER)** and **Bayesian Rule Lists (BRL)**. These algorithms generate unordered or ordered sets of probabilistic rules.

2.2.2 Post-hoc Methods

When complexity of the data, such as raw pixel values of an image or the semantic tokens of a text corpus, or the requirement of state-of-the-art may necessitate use of complex models like Deep Neural Networks (DNNs) or Gradient Boosting Methods (GBMs), ante-hoc methods often prove insufficient. In such scenarios, practitioners turn to post-hoc explainability methods. They approximate the model's behavior or attribute importance to input features to explain why a decision was made.

The taxonomy of post-hoc methods is multi-dimensional and rich, categorized primarily by the scope of explanation, model dependency, and the underlying technique.

2.2.2.1 Scope of Explanation

The first major division concerns the scope of explanation provided: *does the explanation method explain the model's behavior across the entire dataset (global), or does it explain the reasoning behind a single, specific prediction (local)?*

Global Explainability

Global methods aim to provide a holistic view of the model's logic, communicating how features affect predictions on average across the entire data distribution. Some of the well-known explanation methods in this category are:

- **Partial Dependence Plots (PDPs)**: Introduced in [65], PDPs visualize the marginal effect of one or two features on the predicted outcome. They estimate the average prediction for a given feature value by marginalizing over the distribution of all other features. While powerful, PDPs rely on the assumption of feature independence. If features are correlated, the method may integrate over unlikely data points, leading to misleading conclusions.
- **Accumulated Local Effects (ALE)**: Proposed by [13] to address the limitations of PDPs, ALE plots compute the average change in prediction within local intervals of the feature. By accumulating these local effects, ALE provides a more robust estimate of feature influence that respects the joint distribution of the data.

Local Explainability

Local methods focus on explaining a single instance rather than the entire dataset:

- **Individual Conditional Expectation (ICE)**: Introduced in [71], ICE plots the functional relationship for each instance in the dataset separately, rather than averaging them. This visualization exposes the heterogeneity in the model. For example, a feature might have a positive effect on average (similar to PDP) but a distinct negative effect for a cluster of instances.
- **Local Interpretable Model-Agnostic Explanations (LIME)**: Introduced by [173], LIME approximates the complex, non-linear decision boundary of a black box model with a simple linear model locally around the prediction. It generates a dataset of perturbed samples (e.g., by occluding parts of an image), weights them by proximity, and fits a sparse linear surrogate. The weights of this surrogate serve as the explanation. LIME is widely used but can suffer from instability due to random sampling.
- **Shapley Additive exPlanations (SHAP)**: Lundberg and Lee [124] introduced SHAP in 2017. SHAP assigns each feature an importance value based on its Shapley value, the average marginal contribution of a feature value across all possible coalitions of features. SHAP provides a mathematical foundation for feature attribution and includes variants like KernelSHAP (model-agnostic) and TreeSHAP (optimized for decision trees).

2.2.2.2 Model Dependency

The second axis of taxonomy distinguishes methods based on their relationship with the underlying model: *are they model-agnostic or model-specific?*

Model-agnostic Methods

These methods treat the AI model as black-box oracle function. They do not require access to the internal weights, gradients, or parameters. Instead, they learn by querying the model with inputs and observing the outputs. Same explanation method (e.g., LIME) can be used to explain a random forest, a support vector machine (SVM), or a neural network. This category includes perturbation-based methods like LIME and game-theoretic methods like SHAP.

Model-specific Methods

They are tailored to specific class of algorithms, most notably DNNs and CNNs. These methods require access to the model's internal state, such as gradients of the loss function with respect to the input, the activation maps of convolutional layers, or the learned weights of attention mechanisms. Because they utilize internal information, these methods are often computationally faster than agnostic methods (requiring only a single forward / backward pass) and provide high quality explanations than agnostic methods. Some model-specific explanation methods are gradient-based methods like Grad-CAM [186], Integrated Gradients (IGs) [210], and Layer-wise Relevance Propagation (LRP) [19].

2.2.2.3 Underlying Technique

The third axis of taxonomy categorizes post-hoc methods by the algorithmic mechanism they use to generate explanations: example-based, attribution-based, and surrogate-based.

Example-based Explanations

They rely on cognitive principle that humans often reason by analogy or contrast. Rather than providing a vector of feature weights, these methods explain decisions by presenting influential data points. Some well-known methods in this category are:

- **Counterfactual Explanations**: They provide explanations in the form of "What-if" scenarios, answering the question "What is the smallest change to the input that would flip the prediction to a desired outcome?" Diverse Counterfactual Explanations (DiCE) [146] is a well-known counterfactual explanation method. In the context of loan applications, for a loan applicant denied credit, DiCE might provide multiple actionable paths: "If your income were $10k higher, you would be approved" or "If your credit history were 2 years longer, you would be approved." To be useful, counterfactuals must satisfy specific constraints: they must be proximal (requiring minimal change), sparse (modifying few features), and plausible (respecting the data manifold; e.g., not suggesting a change that leads to an impossible combination like "Age: 2, Qualification: Ph.D.").

- **Prototypes and Criticisms**:

  - Prototypes are instances from training data that are mathematical representatives of a class or a cluster. **ProtoDash** [76], a well-known prototype-based method, selects a weighted set of prototypes from the source data that best approximates the distribution of the target instance or dataset. In complex domains like healthcare, showing a typical historical case of a specific disease can be more communicative to a physician than an abstract feature importance map.
  - **Criticism** complements prototypes. "Criticism" samples are selected to represent edge cases or outliers that are not well-explained by the prototypes, providing a complete picture of the data distribution.

- **Neighborhood Approaches**: These methods explain prediction by analyzing the training data points that most strongly influenced the model's learned parameters. **Influence functions**, a class of neighborhood approaches, are adapted from robust statistics by [102]. They approximate the effect of removing a specific training point on model's loss parameters without the prohibitive cost of re-training. By using the inverse Hessian of the loss function, this method can trace a specific prediction back to the "influential" training images (e.g., identifying that a test image of a wolf was classified as such because of specific training images of wolves in snow). This is important for debugging dataset errors and detecting data poisoning attacks.

Attribution-based Explanations

Attribution methods assign a score to each input feature indicating its contribution to the model's output.

- **Gradient-based Methods**: These are standard model-specific methods for interpreting DNNs leveraging the differentiability of the network.

  - **Saliency maps** [193] compute the gradient of the class score with respect to the input image. This map highlights pixels that, if changed slightly, would have most significant impact on the prediction.
  - **Integrated Gradients (IG)** [210] addresses the saturation problem, where gradients become zero despite a feature being important (e.g., a pixel is fully black, and making it more black does not change the score).
  - **Gradient-weighted Class Activation Mapping (Grad-CAM)** [186], which computes the gradients of the target class flowing into the final convolutional layer rather than the input. These gradients are used to weight the feature maps, producing a heatmap that identifies the regions of the image driving the decision. It is applicable to any CNN architecture.

- **Perturbation-based Methods**: These model-agnostic methods estimate importance of features by actively modifying the input and observing the output changes. Examples: LIME, Anchors.
- **Game Theory-based Methods**: Lundberg and Lee [124] unified various attribution methods under the framework of cooperative game theory: SHAP, KernelSHAP, and TreeSHAP.

Surrogate-based Explanations

Surrogate methods seek to replace or approximate the complex *black-box* model with a *white box* model, either locally or globally.

- **Rule Extraction**: These methods extract symbolic rules from neural networks to make their logic explicit.
  - **TREPAN** [48] extracts decision trees from trained neural networks. Unlike standard decision tree induction, TREPAN uses the neural network as an oracle to label synthetic examples, allowing it to explore decision boundary more thoroughly than the limited training data would permit. It translated the network's knowledge into a hierarchical rule set.
  - **Deep Neural Networks Rule Extraction via Decision Trees (DeepRED)** [239] extracts rules from DNNs layer-by-layer. It simplifies the network by discretizing activation values and generating rules for each hidden layer, chaining them together to form a complete rule set from input to output.
- **Distillation**: Knowledge distillation, typically used for model compression, is also a powerful tool for interpretability. **Born-again networks** [66], for instance, demonstrated that a complex teacher model can train a student model of identical or simpler architecture to match its output distribution. By training a transparent student to mimic a high-performance black-box, practitioners can create a model that is both accurate and inherently interpretable.

This shows the methodological diversity within XAI and how methods differ not only in purpose but also in their reliance on model assumptions and explanatory mechanisms. While the majority of contemporary work emphasizes post-hoc strategies to handle complex black-box models, the taxonomy in Fig. 2.2 is not exhaustive and should be seen as a high-level overview rather than a definitive catalog.

Explanation methods, however, bring their own problems. Most current XAI techniques generate one-shot explanations, treating explanation as a destination rather than a process. Yet, as users puzzled by a model's behavior know, explanation is rarely a one-off affair [85]. Miller [140] defines the recommendation-driven paradigm as the dominant approach in XAI, where a system first presents what it considers the best answer or decision, the *recommendation*, and then provides an explanation to persuade the user to accept it. The paper argues that this paradigm is *dead* in many decision-making contexts because it is counter-productive. Current XAI methods often offer an opinion and then insist it is correct. This approach is flawed because it ignores human cognitive processes such as abductive reasoning (forming and testing hypotheses) and reduces user control. The result is poor trust calibration (both over- and under-reliance on the AI) and limited cognitive engagement with the explanations themselves (Table 2.1).

Definition: Interpretability Versus Explainability

Interpretability is an inherent property of a model that makes its predictions directly understandable and faithful to its internal logic (e.g., white-box models such as decision trees or logistic regression).

Explainability relies on external methods to approximate and communicate the behavior of a black-box model. These explanations are not fully accurate but can still provide useful insights into how the model behaves.

2.3 Introduction to AI Model Rating

This idea of rating was introduced in [201, 202] to assess automated machine translation systems with respect to gender bias, accompanied by visualization methods to communicate these ratings to users [26] and user studies examining how such ratings influence perceived trust [24]. The core idea, illustrated in Fig. 2.3, was to distinguish whether biased behavior originated within the AI system itself or was merely a reflection of bias present in the input data. If a system produced biased output even when given unbiased input, the bias was attributed to the model. Conversely, if biased behavior appeared only in response to biased input, the system was characterized as data-sensitive rather than intrinsically unfair. Systems that remained unbiased under both conditions exhibited a compensatory effect.

This view of rating was subsequently generalized beyond translation to other black-box AI services. In particular, the same testing philosophy was used to rate dialog systems (chatbots) based on their behavior with respect to a configurable set of trust-related issues, such as bias (B), abusive language (AL), conversation complexity (CC), and information leakage (IL), for which automated checkers exist in the literature [51, 80, 88]. As illustrated in Fig. 2.4, these systems take as input the chatbot under evaluation (or historical interaction data), the set of issues to be tested, and user profiles that assign relative importance to different issues (e.g., privacy-conscious users). While effective in exposing sensitivity to

Table 2.1 Goals of XAI, their descriptions, and main target audience (based on [14, 227])

XAI Goal	Description of the goal	Main target audience
Trustworthiness	Degree of confidence a model will behave as expected when solving a problem	Domain experts, users of the model affected by decisions
Causality	Finding cause-effect relationships among variables to increase model comprehensiveness	Domain experts, managers, executive board members, regulatory entities/agencies
Transferability	Uncovering boundary constraints of models to assess their applicability in other cases	Domain experts, data scientists
Informativeness	Distinguishing between the human decision-making problem and the one solved by the model, including its inner mechanisms	All
Confidence	Robustness and stability of a model, including its operating regime	Domain experts, developers, managers, regulatory entities/agencies
Fairness	Prohibiting unfair or unethical use of model results; ensuring ethical analysis and illumination of results affecting relations	Users affected by model decisions, regulatory entities/agencies
Accessibility	Involving (non-technical) end users in the AI modeling process	Product owners, managers, users affected by model decisions
Interactivity	Level of interaction between end users and XAI models to improve use	Domain experts, users affected by model decisions
Privacy awareness	Informing users about possible privacy breaches and their implications	Users affected by model decisions, regulatory entities/agencies

data, models, and users, these early rating approaches relied on distributional comparisons and issue-specific checks without explicitly modeling the causal mechanisms through which protected attributes influence outcomes.

This limitation motivates a closer connection between rating, fairness metrics, and causal analysis, rather than treating them as separate evaluation tools. Besides accuracy metrics, which measure predictive performance, another way to understand model behavior is through fairness metrics. These capture whether AI models show discrepancies across classes of

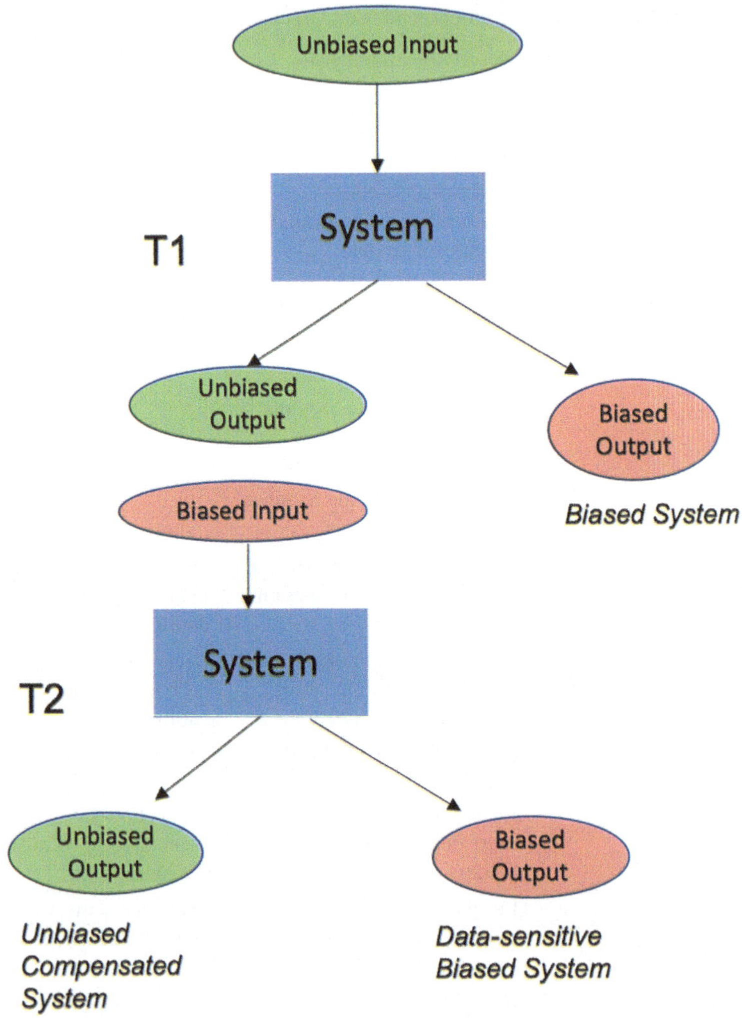

Fig. 2.3 An early two-stage approach for rating AI services based on their behavior under unbiased and biased inputs [202]. The generated trust ratings (labels) are: **a** Biased Systems, **b** Unbiased Compensated System, or **c** Data-sensitive Biased System

protected attributes. Fairness metrics go beyond accuracy by communicating differences in treatment that accuracy alone cannot reveal. Rating methods introduced in [200] and the causality-based rating approach proposed in [111] extend this idea further. These methods quantify AI model behavior using statistical and causal approaches (the latter in the causal framework), and derive ratings from these quantified values to compare models under different input conditions (e.g., varying protected attributes, model behavior under perturbations). The method also provides two baselines: random and biased models, to contextualize ratings.

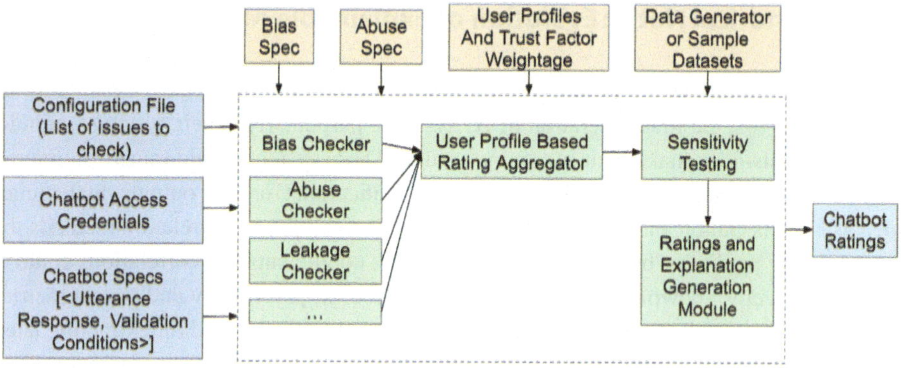

Fig. 2.4 Architecture of a chatbot rating approach introduced in [203]. The chatbot is tested on a set of configurable *issues*, like bias, abuse, information leakage and dialog complexity, via corresponding checkers. The results are aggregated based on user profiles and statistical sensitivity considerations to generate trust rating values (labels) for the chatbot under evaluation settings

This helps users select the right model for a task based on the data at hand, thereby supporting the decision-making process. Chapter 3 explores the rating method in more depth, including the causal setup used to compute ratings across models.

Why do we need rating?

Accuracy and fairness metrics alone are not enough to decide which model to trust in practice. Users, especially in regulated settings like finance, need a simple and standardized way to compare models across different input settings. Ratings serve this role by summarizing complex model behavior into a form that supports reliable decision-making. As discussed in Sect. 1.4 of Chap. 1, ratings serve as food labels for AI models. They communicate model behavior under different conditions and along different dimensions, such as bias from protected attributes and robustness to perturbations. Just as food labels help consumers choose food based on nutritional requirements or dietary restrictions, ratings help users select the right model for their AI task. Ratings provide quantified metrics for users who want exact scores for debugging, while the automatically generated ratings give high-level scores that allow users to quickly compare different test models. The method also allows users to choose the rating scale they prefer. In addition, it enables testing of hypotheses, validation of these hypotheses through quantification of effects of one attribute on another, and translation of these quantified effects into ratings. The rating method strikes a balance between the flexibility available to the user and the assumptions made by the method, so that the analysis remains focused on a restricted set of hypotheses rather than attempting to test everything.

2.4 Historical Notes: Evolution of Explainable AI

The concern with making AI models interpretable predates the term *explainable AI*. In the 1970s and 1980s, the first generation of AI systems, particularly expert systems, included basic mechanisms to make their reasoning visible. These systems could transform internal rules into natural language, providing users with justifications for their outputs. Statisticians such as Francis Galton and Karl Pearson pioneered regression and correlation methods that were not only predictive but also interpretable [205]: coefficients and correlations could be inspected directly, showing how variables were linked. In psychology and psychometrics, Charles Spearman's 1904 work on factor analysis introduced a method for extracting latent dimensions in test data, with results that could be directly interpreted by researchers. These traditions established the expectation that mathematical models should be transparent and their reasoning open to inspection. During the 1990s and early 2000s, attention shifted toward human-computer interaction and knowledge-driven reasoning [147]. Statistical machine learning began to replace symbolic systems. Models such as decision trees and logistic regression preserved some interpretability, but ensemble methods, support vector machines, and early neural networks shifted the balance toward accuracy at the cost of interpretability. Many papers have frequently noted the inverse relationship, where an increase in model performance often leads to a decrease in interpretability [120]. This trend accelerated with the deep learning revolution of the 2010s [115], where architectures like Convolutional Neural Networks (CNNs) [116], Long Short-Term Memory (LSTM) networks [84], and transformers [223] achieved breakthroughs in vision and language but produced predictions that were not interpretable. The rise of proprietary scoring systems in finance, such as the FICO score [86], reinforced this problem by deliberately concealing algorithms for commercial advantage. Their complexity gave rise to the "black-box problem," and after 2013 there was a noticeable surge in publications calling for interpretability [42].

The mid-2010s marked the birth of the modern XAI movement [15]. In 2015, methods such as Layer-Wise Relevance Propagation (LRP) [19] began to explain neural network predictions by tracing relevance scores back to the input. In 2015, the US Defense Advanced Research Projects Agency (DARPA) launched its XAI program, formally popularizing the term. That year also saw the introduction of Local Interpretable Model-agnostic Explanations (LIME) [173], which explained individual predictions by approximating a black-box model locally with a simpler one. In 2017, Shapley Additive exPlanations (SHAP) [124] provided a unified game-theoretic framework for feature attribution, while Integrated Gradients (IG) [210] offered a new way to assign attribution scores in deep networks. These methods quickly became foundational.

Between the late 2010s and early 2020s, XAI research expanded rapidly, with 2018 often identified as a turning point when the number of publications grew sharply, particularly in finance [15]. During this period, the field shifted away from developing inherently transparent white-box models and instead focused on post-hoc explanation techniques for widely used black-box models such as XGBoost and deep neural networks. SHAP and LIME became the most widely adopted explanation methods in finance [74], frequently applied together to provide both global (model-level) and local (instance-level) explanations. At the same time, critiques of these methods gained traction. Rudin et al. [182] argued that in critical domains, black-box explanations should be abandoned altogether in favor of interpretable models with competitive accuracy. Other studies questioned the reliability of explanation mechanisms such as attention weights [90], while new approaches such as Cohort Shapley values [123] were introduced to better capture fairness in model outputs. A variety of XAI methods appeared, including visualization techniques such as Parallel Coordinate Plots [215] and dimensionality reduction methods like t-SNE [125] and UMAP [134].

Since 2022, the rise of large language models (LLMs) has reshaped the agenda for XAI. Finance-specific models such as BloombergGPT [230] have introduced new challenges, most notably *hallucinations*, where models generate plausible but false information [98]. Recent work has moved toward comprehensive frameworks and toolkits rather than single explanation methods. For example, the SAFE framework (Sustainability, Accuracy, Fairness, Explainability) [59] has been proposed for assessing trust in financial AI, while the KAIRI framework (Key Risk Indicators for AI Risk Management) [69] focuses on model safety. Open-source libraries such as PiML [209] and Aletheia [208] extend support for interpretable models and validation. Legal and ethical requirements are now central to this momentum. The EU's General Data Protection Regulation (GDPR), adopted in 2016 with its "right to explanation," and the EU AI Act of 2024 both mandate transparency for high-risk AI systems.

Current Explainable AI (XAI) approaches suffer from several fundamental shortcomings that limit their effectiveness in real-world decision-making. A primary issue is that most XAI tools are designed for developers, focusing on justifying a model's output rather than serving the diverse needs of all stakeholders, including individual users, regulators, and organizational data scientists [113]. The *recommendation-driven* approach, which presents a single answer and its justification, is often counter-productive as it fails to align with the natural cognitive process of human decision-making, namely, abductive reasoning, where people form and test their own hypotheses [140]. This approach can lead to over- or under-reliance on the AI, as it reduces the user's control and provides static, *one-shot* explanations rather than facilitating an interactive, exploratory process [85]. Furthermore, widely used techniques like SHAP and LIME are effective for explaining why a single prediction was made but are ill-equipped to answer broader, critical questions about a model's overall fairness across subgroups, or its robustness under input perturbations. To address these issues, [140] proposes a hypothesis-driven framework called *Evaluative AI*, where the system does not provide recommendations at all. Instead, it acts as a *machine-in-the-loop* tool that empowers a decision-maker by providing evidence for and against the user's own proposed hypotheses, thereby supporting their natural reasoning process and maintaining their control. Lakkaraju et al. [113], Widener et al. [229] introduce a more concrete, integrated approach called Holistic-XAI (H-XAI), which combines traditional XAI methods with Rating-Driven Explanations (RDE). RDE utilizes a causal framework to explicitly test user hypotheses about system behavior, such as model performance across different groups or sensitivity to small changes in the input data. By integrating these methods, H-XAI creates an interactive, multi-method process that allows different stakeholders to move between instance-level feature attributions and system-level robustness and fairness evaluations, effectively shifting explanation from a static justification to a dynamic exploration.

Looking ahead, several research directions remain open. These include developing domain-specific XAI methods tailored to finance, refining the balance between interpretability and performance, advancing causal approaches that explain cause-and-effect rather than correlations, and designing explanation techniques for generative models and other emerging AI technologies. Taken together, the history of XAI reflects a long trajectory: from rule-based transparency, to the black-box problem, to today's frameworks that seek to balance predictive power with accountability and regulatory compliance.

2.5 Chapter Summary

Overall, this chapter discusses various types of AI models and the methods used to communicate their behavior, while highlighting the following key points:

- White-box models such as logistic regression and decision trees show directly how input factors influence predictions.
- Black-box models such as neural networks and transformers can process inputs at scale, but the path from input to decision is hidden and must be approximated by post-hoc explainers.
- The trade-off is clear: interpretable models provide accountability but have limited scope, while black-box models achieve higher performance and generalizability at the cost of transparency.
- Modern explainability techniques are organized into ante-hoc (intrinsic) and post-hoc categories, further divided by scope (local v/s global), model dependency, and methodology (attribution, example-based, surrogate models).
- Explanation goals include trustworthiness, fairness, confidence, interactivity, and privacy awareness, but most current methods still provide static, one-off explanations that do not support iterative reasoning.
- Ratings were introduced as a complementary tool, extending beyond accuracy and fairness metrics to quantify and communicate AI robustness and bias across different input conditions.

Rating AI Models for Robustness

3

There's only a limited amount that AI researchers can do to influence the evolution of global policy on AI. We can point to possible applications that would provide economic and social benefits; we can warn about possible misuses such as surveillance and weapons; and we can provide roadmaps for the likely path of future developments and their impacts. Perhaps the most important thing we can do is to design AI systems that are, to the extent possible, provably safe and beneficial for humans.

—Stuart Russell, Human Compatible: Artificial Intelligence and the Problem of Control, 2019

3.1 Principles of Causality

Causality is the study of cause and effect. It seeks to identify which variables directly influence an outcome, rather than those that merely occur with it (correlations). A user of an AI system may ask why a model produced a certain prediction, why it appears biased, or what factors truly drive its behavior. Causality provides a formal language to express and test such questions. It distinguishes between what *co-occurs* and what *produces* an effect. One common phrase one hears when coming across the term causality for the first time is "*Correlation is not causation.*" Correlation describes statistical association, two variables changing together, without implying that one affects the other. Causation establishes direction: from cause to effect. This distinction is crucial in critical domains such as finance, where models trained only on correlations can depend on features that are correlated with outcomes but not causally responsible for them, a phenomenon known as *spurious association*, where apparent relationships arise from hidden or confounding factors rather than actual causal links. For example, an AI-based credit-scoring model may learn that applicants from certain postal codes default more often and penalize them, even though the postal code is only correlated with long-term economic inequality rather than causing default risk. Such confounding leads to misleading or unfair decisions, making a causal language necessary to represent these scenarios accurately.

The Ladder of Causation. Causality can be thought of as a three-rung ladder, introduced by Judea Pearl [160], that describes the levels of reasoning required to move from simple observation, to estimating the effects of interventions, and finally to estimating counterfactual outcomes.

K. Lakkaraju and B. Srivastava, *Assessing, Explaining, and Rating AI Systems for Trust*, Synthesis Lectures on Computer Science,
https://doi.org/10.1007/978-3-032-21039-5_3

- **Level 1–Association (Seeing)**. The lowest rung deals with correlations and statistical dependencies. Here, we can answer questions like "How are the features in a system statistically associated?" Traditional machine learning largely operates at this level: it identifies patterns between different features. In credit risk assessment, a model might learn that applicants from a certain postal code default more often, but that observation alone says nothing about why.
- **Level 2–Intervention (Doing)**. The second rung asks what happens when we change something in the system. This is the realm of experiments and controlled interventions, where we ask "How does the outcome change if we act on a variable?" In credit risk assessment, this might mean increasing the loan amount or modifying an applicant's features to see how the model's prediction changes.
- **Level 3–Counterfactuals (Imagining)**. The highest rung requires reasoning about alternate realities: what would have happened under different circumstances. It asks "What would the outcome have been if a specific variable had taken a different value?" For example: Would this applicant have been approved if they were of a different gender but identical in every other respect? Such a question cannot be answered directly in the real world.

Together, these three levels: *seeing, doing, and imagining*, form the intellectual ladder that moves us from mere observation to reasoning about counterfactuals. AI models that rely only on correlations among features may perform well in one environment but fail to generalize when deployed in another. Figure 3.1 illustrates this phenomenon: the model learns to associate background context (e.g., home or forest) with the class label, rather than focusing on the causal features of the subject in the foreground. Consequently, when the background distribution shifts, the model mis-classifies the foreground entity even though its intrinsic, task-relevant attributes remain unchanged. In causal inference, this challenge of transferring learned relationships from a source domain (training environment) to a target domain (test environment) is known as the *transportability problem* [130]. Causal transportability refers to the ability to carry causal knowledge or effect estimates across domains with differing data distributions. Building trustworthy AI systems thus requires moving beyond correlation-based learning to identify and model the underlying causal mechanisms that govern system behavior.

Definition: Interventions

An **intervention**, denoted by $do(T = t)$, represents the act of externally setting the treatment variable (T) to a specific value t while breaking all incoming causal links to T. It is the formal operation used to distinguish correlation from causation, as defined in Pearl's do-calculus.

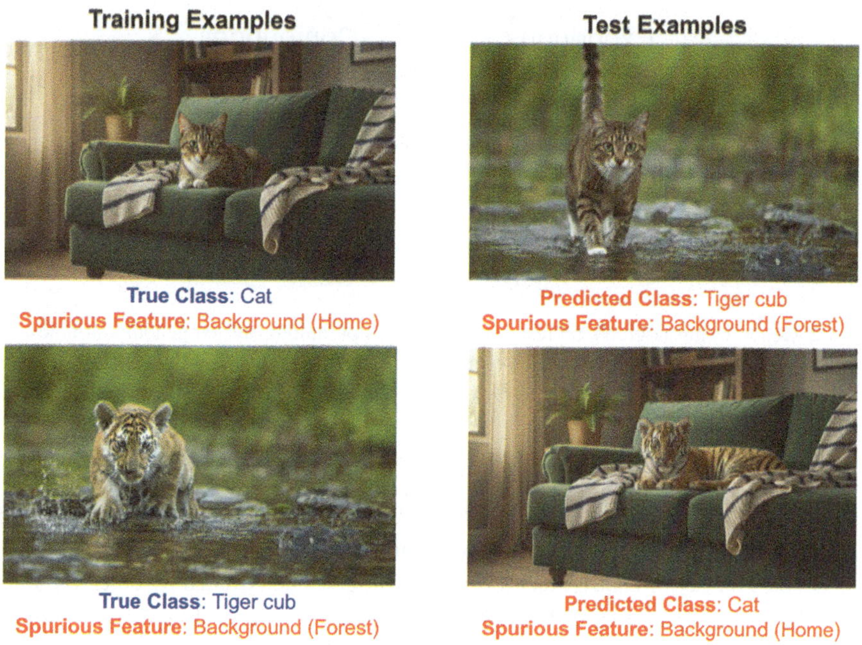

Fig. 3.1 Example of spurious correlation in image classification. During training, the model learns to associate the class label (cat or tiger cub) with the background rather than the animal itself. At test time, when the background–label correlation changes, the model fails, mis-classifying the cat in the forest as a tiger cub and the tiger cub indoors as a cat. This illustrates how reliance on non-causal features leads to wrong predictions (Tested on October 23, 2025 at 11:43 AM EST.)

3.2 Causal Setup for Rating

A causal model formally specifies how variables in a system influence one another. In the context of assessing and rating AI systems, such a model enables us to reason about how different factors, including protected attributes, affect model predictions, and whether those effects are legitimate or spurious. This section presents the general causal setup and illustrates it using a credit risk assessment example.

3.2.1 General Causal Model

A causal model can be formally represented as a *Structural Causal Model (SCM)* defined by the tuple:

$$M = \langle U, V, F, P(U) \rangle$$

where:

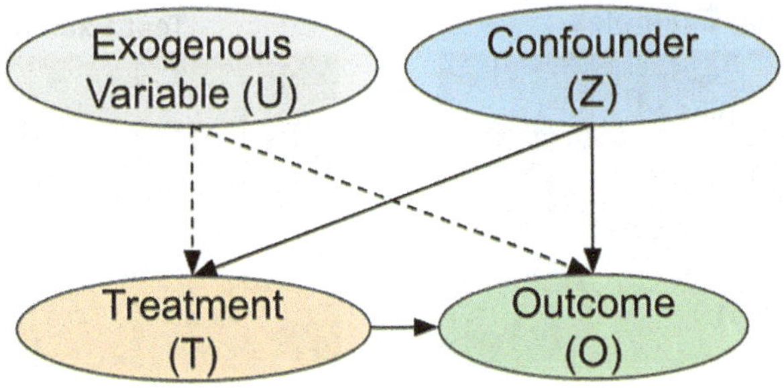

Fig. 3.2 General causal graph representing relationships among an exogenous variable (U), a confounding variable (Z), a treatment or input variable (T), and the outcome (O). Solid edges denote observable causal dependencies, while dashed edges represent unobserved confounding paths through U

- U denotes the set of *exogenous* (unobserved) variables representing background factors external to the model that may introduce confounding.
- V denotes the set of *endogenous* (observed) variables determined by other variables in $U \cup V$. In the general case, $V = \{Z, T, O\}$, where Z is a confounding or contextual attribute, T is the treatment or input variable, and O is the outcome.
- $F = \{f_i\}$ represents the set of *structural functions*, one for each $V_i \in V$, defining how each variable is generated from its parents and corresponding exogenous component:

$$V_i = f_i(\text{Pa}(V_i), U_i)$$

- $P(U)$ is the joint probability distribution over the exogenous variables, capturing uncertainty external to the system.

An SCM can be represented graphically as a *causal graph* or *Directed Acyclic Graph (DAG)*, $\mathcal{G} = (\mathcal{V}, E)$, where $\mathcal{V}$ denotes the set of nodes (variables) and E the set of directed edges representing causal dependencies among them. A directed edge $(T \rightarrow O) \in E$ indicates that T has a direct causal influence on O as defined by the structural function f_O. The absence of an edge implies conditional independence between variables according to the model structure.

Figure 3.2 provides a general schematic of this formulation. Here, the exogenous variable U influences both the treatment T and the outcome O, introducing unobserved confounding. The observed confounder Z can also influence both T and O, creating what is known as a *backdoor path* between them. A backdoor path is any route in the causal graph from T to O that begins with an arrow pointing into T (for example, $T \leftarrow Z \rightarrow O$). Such a path allows information to "flow" from T to O through Z, even if T does not truly cause O, thereby inducing a spurious association. Unless this path is blocked, typically by conditioning on or adjusting for Z, the estimated effect of T on O will combine the true causal influence with bias introduced by confounding. This notion of identifying and closing backdoor paths is central to the rating method, which relies on backdoor adjustment methods to isolate the true effect of treatments on model outcomes. Solid edges in the figure represent direct causal relations among observed variables, while dashed edges represent unobserved confounding through U.

Definition: Confounders and Confounding Effect

A **confounder** (Z) is a variable that causally influences both the treatment (T) and the outcome (O), creating a spurious association between them. This spurious association is known as the **confounding effect**. Confounding opens a *backdoor path* ($T \leftarrow Z \rightarrow O$) that can make the treatment appear to affect the outcome even when no direct causal link exists. In the rating method, protected attributes such as gender or age are treated as potential confounders whose effects are measured through the metric, Deconfounding Impact Estimate (DIE%).

Unobserved confounders can bias causal estimates even after adjustment. Common strategies to mitigate their effect include *sensitivity analysis* [177], which quantifies how strongly an unmeasured confounder would need to influence the treatment to invalidate observed results, and *instrumental variable* methods [10], which use external variables correlated with the treatment but not directly with the outcome to identify causal effects. More recent approaches use latent variable modeling and ML-based methods such as the *sequential deconfounder* [77], which infer hidden confounders from observed data patterns.

Definition: Deconfounding Versus Backdoor Adjustment

Deconfounding refers to the process of removing the influence of confounding variables that affect both the treatment (T) and the outcome (O), thereby allowing one to estimate the true causal effect of T on O. The most common approach is the **backdoor adjustment**, which blocks all backdoor paths between T and O by conditioning on a set of confounders (Z). In the rating method, deconfounding is achieved using techniques such as propensity score matching (PSM), g-computation, or doubly robust estimators.

To ground this formulation, consider a simplified credit risk assessment scenario where the goal is to predict whether a loan applicant is a *good* or *bad* risk. The key variables are:

- Z_1: Gender (protected attribute)
- Z_2: Age (protected attribute)
- T: Credit Amount (treatment)
- O: Predicted Risk (outcome)

Demographic attributes such as *gender* (Z_1) and *age* (Z_2) can influence both the *credit amount* (T) and the model's *predicted risk* (O), thereby creating confounding paths. For instance, if gender (Z_1) influences the approved credit amount (T) and the model's predictions depend on that amount, part of the observed effect of credit (T) on predicted risk (O) may actually arise from gender(Z_1), not from creditworthiness itself. The credit risk causal model in Fig. 3.3 follows the same logic as the general model in Fig. 3.2, but replaces the abstract variables (Z, T, O) with their counterparts specific to this example.

3.2.2 Direct, Indirect, and Confounding Effects

Causal analysis allows us to separate how different variables in a model influence one another, distinguishing true effects from spurious effects. In the general causal model (Fig. 3.2), the treatment T influences the outcome O, but this relationship may also be affected by other variables, both observed (Z) and unobserved (U). Understanding these causal pathways is crucial for assessing whether an AI model is stable or unstable, which forms the foundation of the causal rating method.

Direct Effect

The *direct effect* measures the influence of T on O when other factors, such as Z, are held constant. It corresponds to the solid arrow $T \rightarrow O$ in both Figs. 3.2 and 3.3. In the credit risk example, this represents how changing the approved credit amount (T) affects

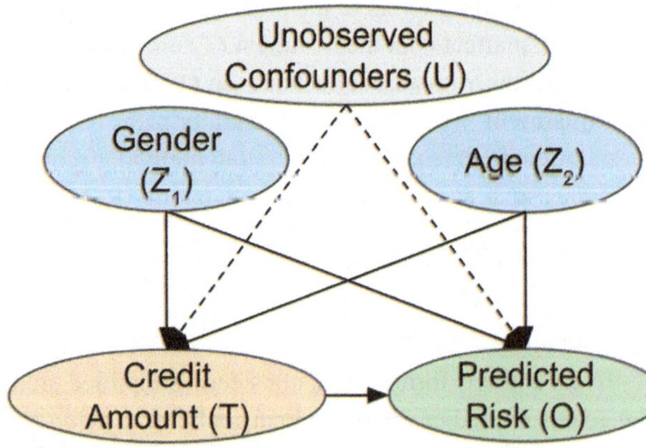

Fig. 3.3 Example causal graph for the credit risk assessment setting. Here, demographic attributes such as gender (Z_1) and age (Z_2) can influence the approved credit amount (T) and, directly or indirectly, the model's predicted risk (O). The figure abstracts these relations into the same structural form as the general causal model in Fig. 3.2

the predicted risk (O) of default, assuming that gender (Z_1) and age (Z_2) remain fixed. If a one-unit increase in the credit amount (T) changes the predicted probability of default by a measurable amount under these fixed conditions, that difference quantifies the direct causal effect of T on O. This pathway represents the valid causal mechanism, where variations in credit amount (T) affect predicted risk (O) solely through credit amount (T) rather than demographic characteristics (Z).

Indirect Effect

The *indirect effect* captures influence that passes through one or more intermediate variables rather than acting directly. In Fig. 3.3, suppose gender (Z_1) or age (Z_2) affects the credit amount (T). For example, older applicants may tend to request smaller loans, or gender may affect approved limits. If the model then uses T to predict risk, part of the effect of these demographic variables on predicted risk flows indirectly through T. Formally, this is the pathway $Z \to T \to O$. Indirect effects are not necessarily undesirable, they depend on the context or the domain. In critical domains such as finance, they become problematic when the mediator (T) transmits effects from protected attributes (Z) that ought not influence the outcome.

Confounding

As discussed earlier, confounding arises when a variable influences both the treatment and the outcome, creating a backdoor path that introduces spurious association. In Fig. 3.2, such confounding occurs through paths like $T \leftarrow Z \to O$ or $T \leftarrow U \to O$. In Fig. 3.3, demographic attributes such as gender (Z_1) or age (Z_2) can confound the relationship between credit amount (T) and predicted risk (O) because they affect both variables. For instance, if certain demographic groups are systematically offered smaller credit amounts (T) and also receive higher predicted risk (O) scores, the apparent link between T and O may partly reflect this demographic influence rather than true effect due to credit amount. To estimate the true causal effect of credit amount (T) on predicted risk (O), these backdoor paths must be *blocked*, typically by conditioning on the confounding variables or through backdoor adjustment methods such as matching or re-weighting.

In summary, the direct effect represents the true causal relationship ($T \to O$), while confounding captures spurious associations arising from unblocked backdoor paths. Depending on the conditioning applied, the rating method can estimate both the direct effect of protected attributes on model outcomes (excluding mediation) and the total effect that includes mediated pathways through variables such as T. It also quantifies the confounding effects introduced by protected attributes, providing a measure of how the confounders affect model predictions.

3.2.3 Quantifying Causal Effects

The goal of causal analysis is to estimate how much a change in one variable *causes* a change in another, rather than merely correlating with it. In our credit risk model (Fig. 3.3), the treatment T represents the approved credit amount and the outcome O is the model's predicted risk. Protected attributes such as gender (Z_1) and age (Z_2) may influence both T and O, introducing bias through the backdoor paths $T \leftarrow Z_1 \rightarrow O$ and $T \leftarrow Z_2 \rightarrow O$. To measure how credit amount causally affects predicted risk (O) rather than just correlating with it, we use the principles of *do-calculus*.

The *do*-operator

The notation $\text{do}(T = t)$ represents an intervention that sets the credit amount T to a fixed value t, as if we were running a controlled experiment. The causal effect of T on O is expressed as:

$$P(O \mid \text{do}(T = t)),$$

meaning the probability of observing each outcome when the credit amount is externally fixed to t, thereby breaking all other incoming influences on T. This operation conceptually "cuts" the arrows pointing into T. For example, those from gender (Z_1) or age (Z_2), so that any remaining association between T and O captures the action causal effect of credit amount (T) on the predicted risk (O).

Backdoor Adjustment

In practice, we cannot always intervene directly, especially with observational data such as historical loan records. Instead, if we can identify and condition on variables that block all backdoor paths from T to O, we can still estimate the causal effect using the backdoor adjustment:

$$P(O \mid \text{do}(T)) = \sum_{Z} P(O \mid T, Z) P(Z).$$

Here, Z represents the set of confounding variables. In our credit risk example, conditioning on gender (Z_1) and age (Z_2) blocks those confounding paths:

$$P(O \mid \text{do}(T)) = \sum_{z_1, z_2} P(O \mid T, z_1, z_2)\, P(z_1, z_2).$$

Intuitively, this means we compare applicants with different credit amounts (T) within the same gender (Z_1) and age (Z_2) groups, so that any difference in predicted risk (O) comes from credit amount (T) rather than from gender (Z_1) or age (Z_2). The resulting estimate represents the causal effect of credit amount (T) on predicted risk (O), free from any demographic bias with respect to the protected attributes (Z) considered.

Frontdoor Adjustment

Sometimes the confounders are unobserved or difficult to measure. If there exists an intermediate variable M that fully mediates the effect of T on O, we can still recover the causal effect through a frontdoor adjustment:

$$P(O \mid \mathrm{do}(T)) = \sum_{M} P(M \mid T) \sum_{T'} P(O \mid M, T')P(T').$$

Here, T' denotes the observed values of the treatment variable across the population, over which the effect is averaged, while T represents the specific treatment level set under intervention. This second summation marginalizes over all possible treatment values to account for their contribution to the outcome distribution.

In the credit scenario, imagine M is a derived feature such as the *credit utilization ratio*, which depends on the requested credit amount and in turn influences predicted risk. Even if the confounding between T and O cannot be directly observed, as long as M transmits all influence from T to O, the frontdoor formula identifies the causal effect through M. This approach conceptually shows how mediation can be leveraged when confounders are unobserved.

Direct and Total Effects

As discussed in Sect. 3.2.2, a variable can influence an outcome both directly and through intermediate variables. Formally, this decomposition can be expressed using the potential outcomes framework [154, 181], which defines causal effects as differences between outcomes under alternate interventions. In this notation, the total effect of a protected attribute Z on an outcome O is written as:

$$\text{Total Effect} = \text{Direct Effect} + \text{Indirect Effect}.$$

Holding T fixed isolates the direct effect, while allowing T to vary naturally captures the total effect, which includes both direct and mediated influences. In the rating method, conditioning choices decide whether the estimate represents the direct effect of an attribute or the total effect that also passes through a mediating variable.

Returning to the causal graph in Fig. 3.3, an unbiased system should exhibit a strong causal link along $T \rightarrow O$ (credit amount influencing risk) and minimal or no influence along $Z_1 \rightarrow O$ or $Z_2 \rightarrow O$. Backdoor adjustment allows us to quantify this by estimating how the predicted risk (O) distribution would change if we could "equalize" gender (Z_1) and age (Z_2) across applicants. If the estimated causal effect of T on O remains stable after adjustment, the model's predictions are robust to variations in protected attributes. If not, differences in Z_1 or Z_2 are contributing to risk scores through confounding, indicating bias. This reasoning forms the empirical basis of the rating method, which uses causal estimates to quantify a model's robustness.

3.3 Quantifying Robustness

In this section, we build on the effects introduced in Sect. 3.2.3 and apply the causality-based methods described in Sect. 3.2.3, together with standard statistical techniques, to define metrics for quantifying the robustness of AI models. These metrics will be used by the rating method to evaluate and compare model behavior. Each metric corresponds to one of the evaluation objectives listed in Table 3.1. The credit risk causal model in Fig. 3.3 serves

Table 3.1 Mapping of evaluation objectives to corresponding metrics and their interpretation in the credit risk setting

ID	Evaluation objective	Metric used and interpretation
E1	Determine whether the protected attribute (Z) directly affects the model outcome (O) even when it has no effect on the treatment (T)	*Weighted Rejection Score (WRS)*: Quantifies direct statistical bias by comparing outcome distributions across protected groups (e.g., gender, age) to test if $Z \rightarrow O$. Lower WRS indicates lower group-level bias
E2	Assess whether the protected attribute (Z) confounds the relationship between treatment (T) and outcome (O)	*Deconfounding Impact Estimate (DIE %)*: Measures confounding bias introduced when Z affects both T and O (backdoor path $T \leftarrow Z \rightarrow O$). Computed as the difference between treatment effects before and after deconfounding. Lower DIE % indicates reduced confounding bias
E3	Evaluate how changes in the treatment (T) causally influence the outcome (O) in the presence of Z	*Average Treatment Effect (ATE)*: Estimates the causal impact of interventions on T (e.g., changes in credit amount) on the outcome O (e.g., predicted risk). Lower ATE value corresponds to a weaker causal effect of the treatment on the outcome
E4	Assess whether the model's performance remains consistent across different treatments (T)	*Accuracy Metrics*: Measure the predictive accuracy of AI model under different treatments

as a running example to illustrate how each metric measures AI models' instability under changing protected attributes (bias) and input perturbations, both of which contribute to its overall robustness.

Definition: Perturbation Versus Treatment

A **perturbation** is a deliberate modification applied to an input feature (text, image, or numerical variable) to examine how the model's predictions change under variation. A **treatment** (T) is the variable whose causal effect on the outcome (O) is to be estimated within the causal model. In the rating method, a perturbation can serve as a treatment when the goal is to measure the isolated causal effect of that perturbation on model predictions or outcome (O).

1. Weighted Rejection Score (WRS)–Statistical Bias. The Weighted Rejection Score (WRS) quantifies whether the model's predicted outcomes differ significantly across groups defined by a protected attribute, such as gender or age. Formally, for each protected attribute $z_i \in Z$, pairwise t-tests are conducted between the outcome distributions $(O|z_i = a)$ and $(O|z_i = b)$ for all a, b group combinations:

$$t_{z_i} = \frac{\text{mean}(O_{z_i=a}) - \text{mean}(O_{z_i=b})}{\sqrt{\frac{s^2_{z_i=a}}{n_{z_i=a}} + \frac{s^2_{z_i=b}}{n_{z_i=b}}}}.$$

At different confidence intervals (CIs), these t-statistics are compared against critical thresholds (t_{crit}). The total WRS is the weighted sum of all rejected null hypotheses:

$$WRS = \sum_i w_i x_i,$$

where x_i is the number of rejections at confidence interval (CI) level i, and w_i is the weight assigned (for example, 1 for 95%, 0.8 for 75%, and 0.6 for 60%).

In credit risk example, if male and female applicants (Z_1) with identical credit profiles show significantly different predicted risk outcomes (O), WRS increases. A high WRS therefore indicates group-level bias in predictions, whereas a lower WRS implies greater statistical parity across protected groups. For instance, if the model predicts an average risk (O) of 0.65 for women and 0.55 for men with the same credit amount (T) and age (Z_2), and this difference is statistically significant, that contributes to a higher WRS value.

Lower WRS ⇒ Lower statistical bias.

2. Deconfounding Impact Estimate (DIE %)–Confounding Bias. While WRS quantifies statistical bias, the rating method treats the protected attribute as a potential confounder, one that may influence both the treatment (T) and the outcome (O), thereby creating spurious associations between them. DIE% measures the extent of this confounding bias by quantifying how much the estimated treatment effect changes after applying a deconfounding.

To compute DIE%, we first estimate the Average Treatment Effect (ATE) using the observed data without adjustment:

$$ATE_0 = E[O|T = i] - E[O|T = 0].$$

Next, we apply a deconfounding method, such as *propensity score matching (PSM)* [178], *g-computation* [151], or *doubly robust estimator* that combines both approaches [21], to obtain an adjusted estimate ATE_m that accounts for the dependence between T and Z.

$$ATE_m = E[O|do(T = i)] - E[O|do(T = 0)].$$

DIE% is then defined as:

$$DIE\% = \big\| ATE_0| - |ATE_m \big\| \times 100.$$

PSM re-creates the conditions of a randomized experiment by pairing treated and untreated units with similar probabilities of receiving the treatment. Formally, we estimate each unit's propensity score $p_i = P(T = 1|Z_i)$ using a logistic or probit model, then match individuals across treatment groups based on p_i. The adjusted outcome difference between these matched pairs provides a deconfounded estimate of the treatment effect.

G-computation, by contrast, models the outcome directly as a function of treatment and confounders,

$$E[O|T, Z] = f(T, Z),$$

using regression or other ML models. We then compute counterfactual predictions by replacing T with its alternate value (0 or 1) for each observation and averaging the difference:

$$ATE_m = E_Z[f(1, Z) - f(0, Z)].$$

This approach explicitly simulates what would happen under intervention, integrating over the observed confounder distribution.

In the credit risk example, consider age (Z_2) as the confounder. Age can influence both the requested credit amount (T) and the model's predicted risk (O). Older applicants may typically request smaller loans and also be assessed as lower risk, while younger applicants may request larger loans and be rated higher risk. As a result, the model learns a strong correlation between loan size and risk, even though part of that relationship arises because of age rather than credit amount itself. This creates the backdoor path $T \leftarrow Z_2 \rightarrow O$. Deconfounding adjusts for age so that applicants of similar age are compared when estimating how changes in requested loan size affect predicted risk. If, after this adjustment, the treatment effect (ATE_m) becomes substantially smaller than before, the DIE% will be high, indicating that age (Z_2) was a major confounder. Conversely, a small DIE% suggests that the apparent link between credit amount (T) and risk (O) is largely causal and not driven by age.

Lower DIE% ⇒ lower confounding bias.

Definition: Statistical Versus Confounding Bias

Statistical bias occurs when the model's predicted outcomes (O) differ across groups defined by a protected attribute (Z), even when other relevant variables are held constant. **Confounding bias** arises when a protected attribute (Z) or another variable influences both the treatment (T) and the outcome (O), creating a spurious association through the backdoor path ($T \leftarrow Z \rightarrow O$). In the rating method, statistical bias is quantified using the Weighted Rejection Score (WRS), while confounding bias is measured using the Deconfounding Impact Estimate (DIE%), which quantifies how the estimated treatment effect changes after adjusting for confounders.

3. Average Treatment Effect (ATE)–Causal Effect under Interventions. ATE quantifies the causal influence of a treatment variable (T) on an outcome (O), providing a general measure of how model predictions respond to interventions on T. It represents the expected change in outcomes when T is set to one value instead of another through a hypothetical intervention, while accounting for potential confounders. Formally, the causal effect is expressed as:

$$ATE = E[O|do(T = i)] - E[O|do(T = 0)].$$

In practice, ATE can be estimated using the same deconfounding methods (PSM, g-computation, or doubly robust approaches), depending on the available data and model structure.

In the credit risk example, an intervention on the requested credit amount (T) represents a hypothetical scenario where an applicant's requested loan size is externally set to a different value while keeping other financial attributes constant. ATE then quantifies the expected change in the predicted risk (O) resulting from this intervention on T. For instance, if $ATE = 0.05$, it indicates that, on average, increasing the requested credit amount (T) by one unit (e.g., from medium to high) raises the predicted probability of default (or risk (O)) by 5 %, after accounting for confounding factors (Z) such as age or gender. Thus, ATE represents the model's overall sensitivity of predicted risk (O) to changes in credit amount (T).

4. Accuracy Metrics–Performance. While other metrics evaluate robustness, the model's accuracy must also be maintained. Standard accuracy measures such as precision, recall, F1-score, and AUC are used to assess overall performance. For example, in the credit risk example, the classifier may perform differently for applicants requesting low versus high credit amounts. Accuracy metrics help quantify these variations in performance under different input settings.

3.4 Rating Workflow

In this section, we describe the workflow of the rating method, which consists of two main stages: *Data-to-Predictions* and *Predictions-to-Ratings*. The first stage, *Data-to-Predictions*, serves as a prerequisite for the rating process. It uses input data, containing protected attributes or their proxies, along with other independent attributes, to generate predictions from the AI model that will later be analyzed in the second stage. The second stage processes the input data and predictions so that they align with the user hypotheses to be tested using the rating method. For example, if our hypothesis is "What is the effect of gender (Z) on the relationship between credit amount (T) and predicted risk (O)?", the rating method applies a fixed causal setup as shown in Fig. 3.4. This causal structure has been used prior work to rate AI models for different tasks, including sentiment analysis systems (SASs) [112], SASs combined with translators as composite systems [107], multi-modal forecasting models [111], and foundation model-based time-series forecasting models [110].

While the same rating method can be adapted to other settings, it has primarily been applied to a specific and limited set of questions defined by the evaluation objectives in Table 3.1 from prior work. In Sect. 4.3 of Chap. 4, we describe how the same causal setup can be extended to evaluate a custom task. We also outline how alternative causal model configurations can be incorporated within the rating framework.

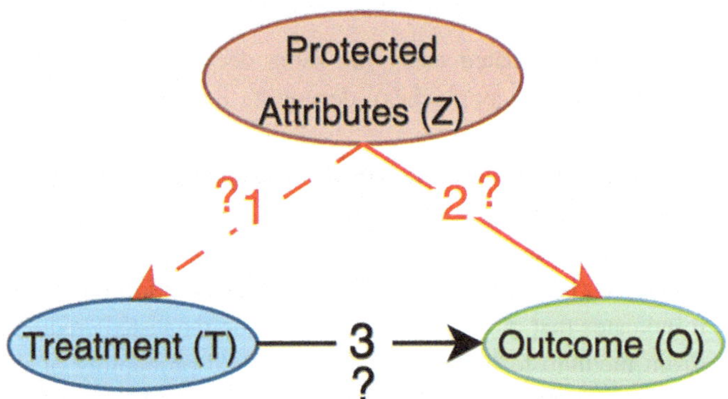

Fig. 3.4 Proposed generalized causal model. The validity of link '1' depends on the conditional distribution ($T|Z$), while the validity of the links '2' and '3' can be tested using the evaluation metrics

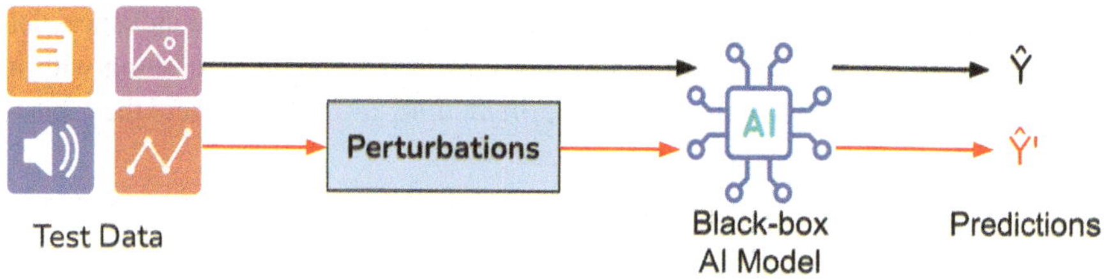

Fig. 3.5 *Data-to-Predictions* workflow for generating predictions using perturbed and unperturbed input data

3.4.1 Data-to-Predictions Workflow

The *Data-to-Predictions* stage serves as a prerequisite to applying the rating method (the second stage) and is illustrated in Fig. 3.5. It corresponds to the process of generating model predictions under both unperturbed and perturbed input conditions. This stage produces the data necessary to assess how interventions affect model outputs or model performance across different data modalities.

The workflow begins with a collection of test data, which may consist of textual, visual, numerical, or multi-modal inputs. Each input is either kept unchanged or perturbed according to the user's objective. Perturbations can take different forms depending on the domain, for instance, modifying words in a text sample, altering pixels in an image, or changing numerical values in a tabular feature. Unperturbed and perturbed inputs are then passed through a black-box AI model to generate corresponding predictions, denoted by $\hat{Y}$ and $\hat{Y}'$. These paired predictions form the empirical basis for estimating causal effects and quantifying robustness within the rating method.

A perturbation can itself be treated as a *treatment* when the objective is to isolate its effect on the model outcome. For example, if data associated with one group defined by a protected attribute experiences a specific kind of noise or perturbation while another group's data remains unaltered, the protected attribute indirectly influences the perturbation applied. In such cases, the perturbation or treatment variable (T) may depend on the protected attribute (Z), creating a causal path $Z \rightarrow T \rightarrow O$. The isolated effect of the perturbation (T) on the outcome can then be measured by intervening on T. Consider a stock-price prediction task where data from one company (representing the protected attribute) contains higher levels of noise than data from other companies. Here, the *company* attribute affects the perturbation applied to the input. The rating method can estimate the isolated effect of such perturbations on the model's predictions by treating the perturbation as a treatment variable and intervening on it.

The objective of this stage is to produce model predictions that capture the effect of applying controlled perturbations to the input data. Protected attributes (Z) or their proxies, along with other independent variables, are included in the data to allow subsequent causal analysis in the next stage.

After the perturbed and unperturbed inputs are passed through the AI model, the resulting predictions ($\hat{Y}'$ and $\hat{Y}$) form the outputs of this stage. These predictions along with input attributes serve as the inputs to the next stage, *Predictions-to-Ratings*, where the robustness metrics are computed and the models are rated.

3.4.2 Predictions-to-Ratings Workflow

Definition: Raw Scores

Raw scores are the numerical outputs obtained for each rating metric before converting them into categorical ratings. They represent the quantitative measurement of model robustness along individual dimensions: statistical bias (WRS), confounding bias (DIE%), and treatment impact (ATE). Raw scores are used to construct a *partial order* of models for each metric, which is later discretized into rating levels (e.g., on a scale of 1 to L), allowing one to compare different AI models easily.

The *Predictions-to-Ratings* stage constitutes the core analytical phase of the rating method. It takes as input the predictions generated in the previous stage and performs statistical and causal analysis to quantify the deconfounded impact of the treatment, the influence of protected attributes on the outcome (statistical bias), and the effect of confounders on the relationship between the treatment and the outcome (confounding bias) across the tested AI models. The workflow, shown in Fig. 3.6, describes how raw scores are computed for each metric and then converted into partial and final ratings.

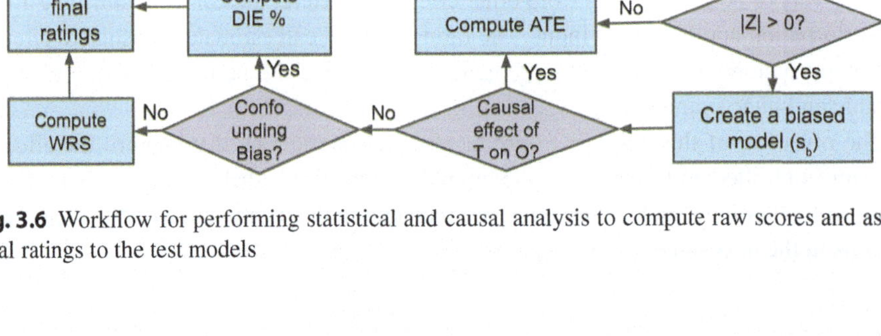

Fig. 3.6 Workflow for performing statistical and causal analysis to compute raw scores and assign final ratings to the test models

This stage begins with a dataset containing model predictions ($\hat{Y}$ and $\hat{Y}'$), protected attributes (Z), the treatment variable (T), which may represent the type of perturbation or another input attribute depending on the user's objective, and outcomes (O). Each AI model S_i in the test set is evaluated independently using the same causal setup shown in Fig. 3.4. For each model, raw scores are computed using either of the three primary metrics, based on the user objective: (1) Weighted Rejection Score (WRS) for direct statistical bias, (2) Deconfounding Impact Estimate (DIE%) for confounding bias, and (3) Average Treatment Effect (ATE) for impact of treatment (T) on the outcome (O) after intervention. These metrics quantify different aspects of model robustness as discussed in Sect. 3.3.

Predictions-to-Ratings Workflow

The workflow illustrated in Fig. 3.6 proceeds through the following steps:

Step 1. Input preparation. For each test model S_i, the method begins with the dataset containing predictions ($\hat{Y}$ and $\hat{Y}'$), protected attributes (Z), treatment variable (T), and outcome (O). The treatment variable can represent a perturbation type or another user-defined feature whose causal influence is to be measured.

Step 2. Check for direct influence of protected attributes. The first check determines whether the protected attributes (Z) directly affect the model outcome (O). If $Z \rightarrow O$, the method computes the *Weighted Rejection Score (WRS)*, which measures statistical bias by testing whether different demographic groups receive significantly different predictions. In the credit risk context, this corresponds to checking if applicants of different genders or ages receive systematically higher or lower predicted risk scores despite having comparable financial profiles.

Step 3. Check for confounding effects. If the protected attributes influence both the treatment and the outcome ($T \leftarrow Z \rightarrow O$), bias may arise through confounding. In such cases, the method computes the *Deconfounding Impact Estimate (DIE%)*, which quantifies how much the estimated treatment effect changes after adjusting for confounders. In the credit risk example, this would indicate whether the relationship between credit amount (T) and predicted risk (O) shifts substantially after controlling for gender or age (Z). A high DIE% indicates strong confounding bias, while a low DIE% suggests that demographic attributes (Z) have limited indirect effect on the outcome (O).

Step 4. Estimate causal effect of treatment. Next, the method examines whether the treatment (T) causally influences the outcome (O). If this effect exists, the *Average Treatment Effect (ATE)* is computed to capture the average change in the outcome resulting from a change in the treatment, after removing the influence of confounders through deconfounding. In the credit risk case, this represents how the predicted risk (O) changes, on average, when the requested credit amount (T) increases from one level (e.g., low) to another (e.g., medium).

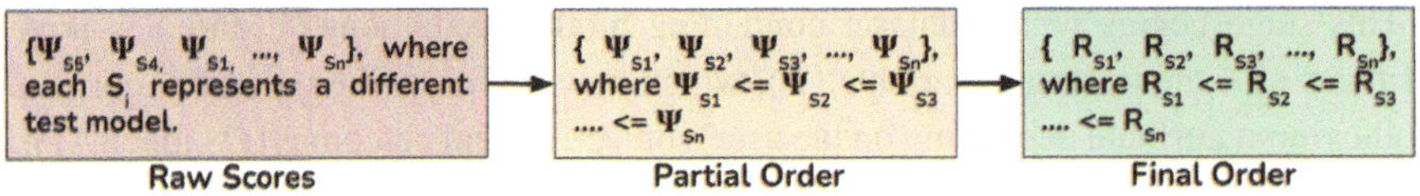

Fig. 3.7 Figure showing how raw metric scores are used to construct a partial order of raw scores and derive the order of final rating

Step 5. Compute raw scores and construct partial order. For each metric, WRS, DIE%, and ATE, a raw score is obtained for every model. These scores are then used to construct a *partial order* that compares models across individual metrics. For example, when comparing two credit risk models, S_1 and S_2, based on the statistical bias they exhibit, the model with a lower WRS would appear earlier in the partial order, indicating better fairness relative to the others.

Step 6. Assign final ratings. The raw metric values are discretized into rating levels (e.g., on a scale of 1–3) based on user-defined thresholds or rating level, L. The ratings are then used to produce a *final order*, which rates or ranks the models according to their overall robustness from more robust to least robust.

In summary, using the causal structure shown in Fig. 3.4 and the metrics introduced in Sect. 3.3, this stage transforms model predictions into raw scores and subsequently into ratings, as shown in Fig. 3.7.

Why Rating Matters: Numerous methods now exist to measure and quantify robustness in AI models, yet these approaches often operate in isolation and lack a common basis for comparison. The causality-based rating method provides a unified setup that allows model comparison under a causally grounded experimental setup. It not only quantifies the direct and confounding effects among inputs, protected attributes, and outcomes but also evaluates models across multiple dimensions of robustness, including bias and model stability. Furthermore, the two default baselines, random and biased, within a shared causal setup allow test models' robustness to be compared objectively, independent of domain or data modality. In domains such as finance, where decisions are tightly linked to regulatory and ethical constraints, such a framework helps identify not only whether a model performs well but also why it behaves as it does.

3.5 Historical Notes: Evolution of Causality

The trajectory of Machine Learning (ML), especially in critical domains such as finance and healthcare, has long been driven by correlational techniques situated at the lowest level of cognitive reasoning, the Rung of *Association* [160]. Although highly effective in maximizing predictive accuracy, such models fail under shifts in data distribution, exposing their lack of causal understanding. This limitation motivated the pursuit of mechanism-based reasoning, where AI systems must not only predict but also explain why an outcome occurs and anticipate the effects of interventions [160]. The emergence of causal inference frameworks, notably Structural Causal Models (SCM) [160], the *do*-calculus [160], and counterfactual reasoning [158], provided formal mathematical foundations for transitioning AI evaluation from statistical performance to robustness-based guarantees [160]. However, the fundamental engineering challenge persists: observational data alone are insufficient to infer new interventions, requiring explicit modeling of underlying causal mechanisms [6].

Early efforts to establish causal relations predate modern AI. In epidemiology, Sir Austin Bradford Hill's 1965 criteria [55, 82], including *temporality* and strength of *association*, were used to argue for the causal link between smoking and lung cancer. While influential, these qualitative criteria were inadequate for modern multivariate, observational data [55]. The realization that major scientific discoveries could emerge without controlled experiments, such as in plate tectonics or evolution, made clear the need for formal methods distinguishing interventions from observations [160, 180]. This led to the mathematical formalization of causality, culminating in Judea Pearl's *Ladder of Causation* [160], which defines three levels of reasoning: association ($P(Y|X)$), intervention ($P(Y|\text{do}(X))$), and counterfactuals ($P(Y_{x'}|X = x)$).

Pearl's SCM framework [160] provides a formal mechanism-based approach separating causal assumptions from statistical observations. Its graphical foundation, Directed Acyclic Graphs (DAGs) [45], allows representation of causal dependencies and facilitates the identification of confounders, mediators, and colliders using the principle of d-separation [160]. The *do*-calculus [160] extends this reasoning, providing algebraic rules for identifying causal effects from observational data. Together, SCM and *do*-calculus form the backbone of modern causal analysis, supporting advanced tasks such as mediation analysis, attribution, transportability, and meta-synthesis.

Parallel to SCM, the Potential Outcomes Framework (POF) or Rubin Causal Model (RCM) [181], originating from Neyman's 1923 work [154], defines causal effects through hypothetical outcomes under alternative treatments [181]. Its central challenge, the "fundamental problem of causal inference," arises because only one potential outcome per unit can be observed [181]. SCMs and POF were later unified under Pearl's general theory of causation [161], with SCM providing graphical and logical completeness for counterfactual reasoning beyond POF's algebraic assumptions [18]. This evolution, from Hill's qualitative heuristics to Rubin's algebraic model and Pearl's graphical SCM, marked a progressive formalization of causal reasoning [180].

In the 1980s through the early 1990s, Truth Maintenance Systems (TMS) [56] expanded the scope of rule-based and logic-driven inference. Developed to help expert systems keep track of how conclusions were derived, a TMS recorded both facts and the reasons supporting them. When new evidence contradicted earlier assumptions, the system could withdraw or revise the affected conclusions. Variants such as the Justification-based TMS (JTMS) [56] and the Assumption-based TMS (ATMS) [53] introduced ways to reason with alternative assumptions and parallel *worlds*. By making dependencies between beliefs explicit, TMSs anticipated later causal modeling frameworks that represent and update relationships among variables in a structured way.

Since real-world causal structures are rarely known, researchers developed causal structure learning (CSL) algorithms to infer them directly from data [79]. Constraint-based approaches such as the Peter-Clark (PC) algorithm [196] infer conditional independencies to recover a causal skeleton, while the Fast Causal Inference (FCI) algorithm [195] generalizes PC to account for latent confounders, producing Partial Ancestral Graphs (PAGs). Nevertheless, CSL remains constrained by assumptions of causal sufficiency, limited samples, and difficulty distinguishing direct from indirect effects [152, 157, 218]. Neural causal discovery, though promising, also struggles to distinguish true causation in finite data regimes [157].

Causal Representation Learning (CRL) extends causal inference into representation spaces, capturing invariant relationships that improve robustness and transferability. Methods like Hybrid Structural Causal Models (HSCMs) [212] and Neural Causal Models (NCMs) [231] integrate causal graphs with neural architectures, aiming to isolate stable causal features while minimizing spurious correlations [40]. These ideas influence fairness and interpretability as well: Counterfactual Fairness (CF) [70, 106] defines a decision as fair if it remains invariant in counterfactual worlds, though its reliance on correct causal models limits real-world application [192].

Causality also forms the theoretical backbone of Explainable AI (XAI). Counterfactual Explanations (CFXs) [225] provide human-aligned interpretability by showing how minimal input changes can alter model outputs. Yet these explanations are often unstable, a phenomenon known as Model Misalignment, since retraining or perturbing the model can invalidate them [92]. The notion of Δ-robustness [36, 92, 93] was introduced to formally assess the stability of CFXs across bounded model perturbations, signaling a shift from generating causal explanations to verifying their robustness under operational conditions.

Miller et al. [139] supports causal inference experiments such as heterogeneous treatment effects and causal structure discovery. Nagpal et al. [148] and Zhang et al. [236] use path-specific effects (PSE) to address discrimination: the former minimizes PSE along unfair paths while maximizing valid ones, while the latter removes direct and indirect discrimination by modifying data to eliminate biased causal pathways. CausalML [41] focuses on estimating treatment effects like Conditional Average Treatment Effects (CATE) for applications such as personalized targeting and uplift modeling, whereas the rating method systematically evaluates AI systems for robustness across tasks. Other frameworks such as [235] and [176] emphasize causal discovery or benchmarking structure learning algorithms but lack the extensibility and evaluation focus of the rating method introduced in [112]. The rating method starts from a predefined causal model and measures the strength of each causal link through quantitative metrics.

Despite these advances, causal methods face practical and philosophical challenges. Building valid causal models requires extensive domain expertise and is computationally expensive [38]. Their validity is tied to the accuracy of assumed structures; unobserved confounders can distort estimates [38]. Moreover, causal formalism alone cannot resolve underlying social or ethical inequities: mathematically correct models can still reproduce biased or incomplete worldviews [38].

These limitations suggest that reliable AI will not emerge spontaneously from scaling data or models. Instead, the path toward trustworthy, causally grounded AI lies in integrating scientific and expert domain knowledge directly into model development and evaluation pipelines. This synthesis, melding formal causal theory with practical domain understanding, defines the next stage in building robust, explainable, and verifiable AI systems.

3.6 Chapter Summary

Overall, this chapter discusses causal methods and rating, while highlighting the following key points:

- Traditional AI evaluation relied on a single accuracy score to indicate performance. As models have become more complex and widely used in sensitive domains like finance, evaluation must now consider multiple dimensions such as robustness, fairness, and interpretability.
- Robustness captures whether an AI model remains stable and reliable when its inputs change, when noise is introduced, or when sensitive attributes vary. A robust model should behave predictably under such conditions, maintaining fairness and stability in its outcomes.
- Causality provides the formal language for reasoning about why outcomes occur, distinguishing cause-effect relationships from correlations. Pearl's *Ladder of Causation*: association, intervention, and counterfactual reasoning, describes the progression from identifying statistical patterns in the data to reasoning about actions and hypothetical alternatives that identify underlying causal mechanisms.
- A causal model is used to represent how factors such as protected attributes, treatments, and outcomes influence one another. It identifies whether changes in a model's predictions arise from causal pathways or from spurious relationships introduced by confounding variables, allowing fair and reliable analysis.
- Causal reasoning differentiates direct, indirect, and confounding effects, making it possible to identify which relationships are truly causal and which arise from spurious correlations or hidden bias.
- Three main metrics operationalize the rating method: (1) *Weighted Rejection Score (WRS)* for group-level statistical bias, (2) *Deconfounding Impact Estimate (DIE%)* for con-

founding bias, and (3) *Average Treatment Effect (ATE)* for sensitivity of predictions to treatments.

- The rating process proceeds in two stages: *Data-to-Predictions*, where models are tested under both unperturbed and perturbed inputs; and *Predictions-to-Ratings*, where statistical and causal analyses convert raw metric values into final ratings that allow users to compare different AI models.
- By grounding robustness in causality, the rating method makes it possible to see how models respond to perturbations and which dependencies make them biased or unstable.

Putting Ratings to Work: Case Studies and Tools 4

Nobody phrases it this way, but I think that artificial intelligence is almost a humanities discipline. It's really an attempt to understand human intelligence and human cognition.

— *Sebastian Thrun*

4.1 Overview of Applications and Tooling

In this section, we motivate the need for a framework like ARC and the importance of tools that assist end-users in selecting appropriate AI models for a given task, based on the characteristics of the available data.

4.1.1 Motivation and Scope

Several statistical approaches have been proposed over the years to assess AI models for fairness [30, 94, 175], and the adversarial machine learning community has developed many tools to test how models behave under input perturbations [37, 145, 155, 159]. These methods have become easily accessible, with many available as open-source frameworks and tools. They have also improved how we measure fairness and instability, but they mostly rely on correlations in the data. They can show that a model's predictions differ across groups or that outputs are sensitive to certain inputs, yet they offer little insight into *why* these patterns arise or how different factors interact to create them. Causal modeling provides a way to address these questions by explicitly representing relationships between attributes and isolating the effects of confounders. Several causality-based fairness metrics have also been proposed in the past; [127] reviews 19 such approaches. However, most rely on rigid causal assumptions, and there is still no unified framework that can quantify multiple robustness metrics within a single causal setup that requires minimal adaptation across settings. Building on this

K. Lakkaraju and B. Srivastava, *Assessing, Explaining, and Rating AI Systems for Trust*, Synthesis Lectures on Computer Science,
https://doi.org/10.1007/978-3-032-21039-5_4

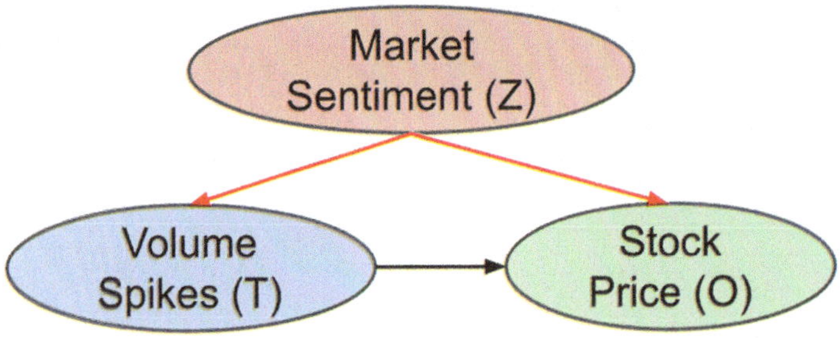

Fig. 4.1 Causal graph showing how market sentiment (Z) confounds the relationship between trading volume spikes (T) and stock price movement (O); modeling this structure allows estimation of the true effect of T on O after deconfounding Z

foundation, ARC offers a structured way to measure model robustness through a causally-grounded experimental setup and to express those measures as ratings that allow comparison of different AI models under varying input conditions, such as perturbations or changes in protected attributes present in the data.

Example. Consider an AI system trained to predict whether a stock's price (O) will rise the next day using trading volume spikes (T) as a signal. If we simply compare average returns following high- (T=1) and low-volume (T=0) days, the estimate also includes the influence of confounding factors such as market sentiment (Z), which affects both trading volume (T) and price movements (O). Statistically, the difference $\mathbb{E}[O \mid T{=}1] - \mathbb{E}[O \mid T{=}0]$ combines the effect of trading volume with the effect transmitted through Z (backdoor path: $T \leftarrow Z \rightarrow O$). A causal model, shown in Fig. 4.1, allows us to adjust for this confounding by estimating $\mathbb{E}[O \mid do(T{=}1)] - \mathbb{E}[O \mid do(T{=}0)]$, which captures how the outcome would change if we could intervene and modify T directly. This distinction separates the true effect of volume spikes from spurious relationships caused by shared conditions such as market sentiment. In practice, many such confounders exist, some observable (Z) and others not (U), and identifying them depends on domain knowledge or understanding of how the data were generated. A similar example will be explained in detail in Sect. 4.2.4.

ARC uses a fixed causal setup to measure the contribution of these confounding effects and to rate different models based on their robustness to them. It also includes baseline predictors, such as a random forecaster and a deliberately biased model, that provide reference points for interpreting the ratings. For instance, if a model performs worse than the biased baseline, it indicates high bias in its learning process; if it performs worse than random, it cannot be considered dependable. For developers, ARC provides detailed metrics values or raw scores; for others, it converts these raw scores into ratings that functions like a *food label* for AI models, reporting how stable and fair a model remains under different input conditions.

At present, there is no general method that allows users to:

- test specific hypotheses about model behavior,
- quantify robustness under those hypotheses, and
- interpret the resulting ratings in relation to meaningful baselines.

Goal of ***AI Rating through Causality (ARC)***

Goal of ARC: to measure AI model robustness through causal reasoning and to help users select the right model for a given task and dataset by providing ratings relative to automatically generated baselines.

4.1.2 Assumptions of the ARC Framework

ARC builds on standard assumptions in causal inference but adapts them to the context of AI model evaluation.

1. ARC assumes a fixed causal structure (shown in Fig. 3.4) under which the outcome-protected attribute discrepancy is computed using a statistical test (e.g., a t-test). Based on the data, this setup allows us to determine whether the treatment is non-uniformly distributed with respect to the protected attribute, that is, whether the treatment depends on the protected attributes considered. This causal formulation satisfies the four user objectives outlined in Table 3.1, providing a limited but easy-to-use and generalizable framework. Although ARC focuses on this basic setup, other causal structures are also possible. For instance, one could include mediators or decompose effects into direct and indirect components, as described in Sect. 3.2.2. Once this setup is defined, AI models can be evaluated and rated alongside the random and biased baselines, which makes the framework naturally extensible.
2. ARC assumes that the relevant confounders are either observed or can be approximated through measurable proxies. Additional tests such as Rosenbaum's sensitivity analysis [178] can be used to estimate how sensitive the causal analysis is to unobserved confounders. ARC, to keep the framework simple, does not include this step by default, but it can be easily integrated into the workflow if required.
3. ARC assumes that users provide a dataset prepared in accordance with the framework's causal setup. Specifically, the data should include: (i) the treatment variables to be analyzed or intervened on, (ii) the protected attributes or potential confounders, and (iii) the outcome variable, which may represent the model's direct predictions or a derived measure such as the residual (difference between the ground truth and the predictions) that serves as a proxy for model performance. Integrating large or custom-trained models

directly into the framework is often impractical, as users may wish to evaluate their own models, including LLMs or proprietary architectures, on data of their choice.

These assumptions are practical in most real-world settings. They define the conditions under which ARC's analysis can be meaningfully interpreted as causal estimates of model robustness, measuring fairness and stability across AI models.

4.1.3 Tooling and Implementation

ARC's rating method and the metrics it uses were discussed in detail in Chap. 3, and the framework's underlying assumptions were outlined in Sect. 4.1.2. The ARC tool, whose interface is shown in Fig. 4.2, was built on the principles of this framework. It is implemented using the Django web framework, which provides an integrated environment for both front-end and back-end development. The front-end uses standard HTML, CSS, and JavaScript components to render dynamic visualizations of metric outputs and Pareto results, while the back-end handles metric computations, database management, and interaction with the metric modules. The main features of the tool are as follows:

1. **Demonstration of ARC's capabilities**: The tool showcases ARC's ability to rate AI models for tasks spanning binary classification, sentiment analysis, group recommendation, and time-series forecasting, each differing in complexity. These case studies are discussed in detail in Sect. 4.2.
2. **Trade-off exploration**: It allows users to explore the trade-off between model performance and robustness using Pareto-optimality analysis (shown in Fig. 4.2b. This helps users identify which models best align with their deployment goals, depending on whether accuracy or robustness is prioritized.
3. **Custom data support**: Users can upload their own datasets prepared according to the specifications outlined in Assumption 3 (Sect. 4.1.2) and structured as shown in Table 4.1. Once uploaded, the tool applies ARC's robustness metrics to evaluate models with respect to the evaluation objectives (E1–E3) listed in Table 3.1.

4.2 Case Studies

Table 4.2 summarizes the tasks, datasets, attributes, evaluation metrics, and AI models implemented in the ARC tool. In this section, we describe how the rating method can be applied across these different tasks and how each of them differs in terms of task objectives and data characteristics, while still fitting within the same causal framework. Although the tasks, ranging from binary credit risk classification to sentiment analysis, group recommendation,

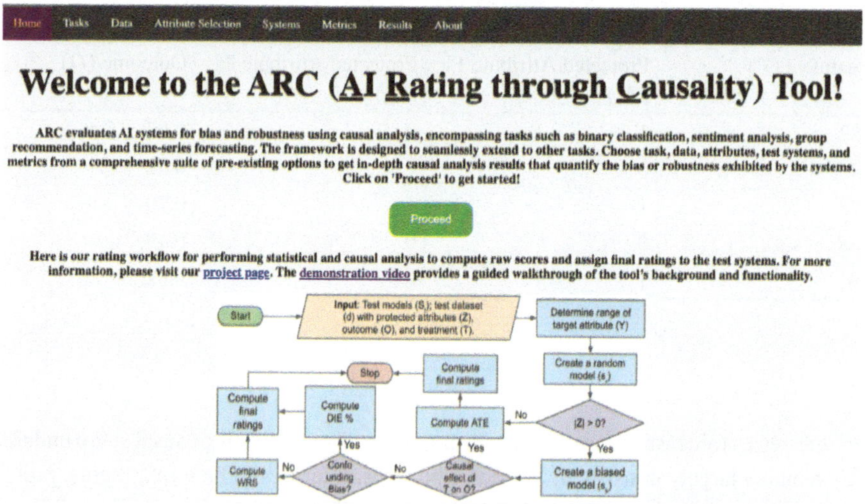

(a) ARC homepage displaying the workflow and task selection interface.

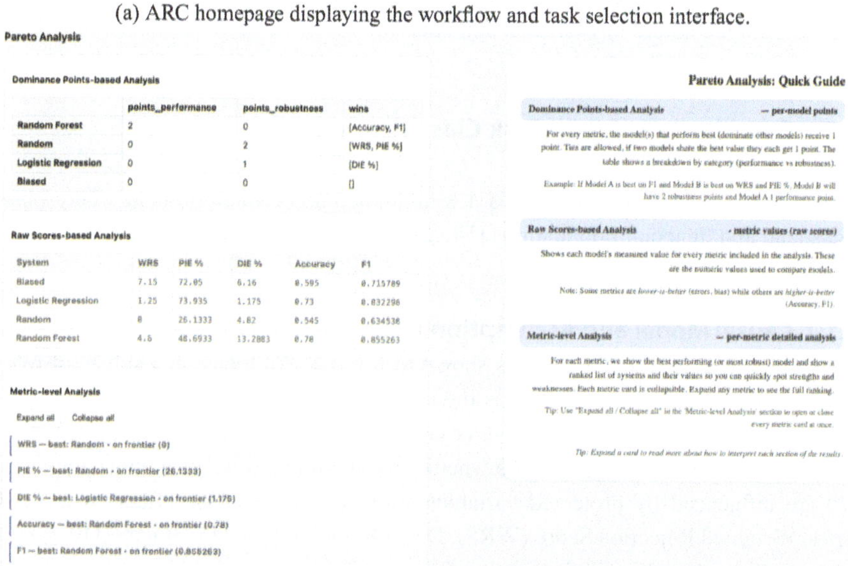

(b) Pareto analysis results showing dominance, raw scores, and metric-level views.

Fig. 4.2 Snapshots of the ARC tool: **a** homepage for task configuration and **b** Pareto analysis interface showing multi-metric evaluation results

Table 4.1 Example structure of input data expected by ARC

Treatment (T)	Protected Attribute 1 (Z_1)	Protected Attribute 2 (Z_2)	Outcome (O)
0.82	1	0	0.67
0.45	0	1	0.52
0.73	1	1	0.70
0.38	0	0	0.49
0.91	1	0	0.82
...	...	...	...

and time-series forecasting, are distinct in structure and modality, the causal setup underlying ARC remains largely consistent. We describe the similarities in how treatments, protected attributes, and outcomes are modeled across these settings, as well as the key differences that arise from the nature of each task and dataset.

4.2.1 Case Study 1: Credit Risk Classification

Binary credit risk classification task is a well-studied and critical domain where bias has direct social and financial implications [54, 101, 137].

4.2.1.1 Causal Model and Assumptions

The causal model used for this task is shown in Fig. 4.3. We focus on a subset of relevant variables: the *Credit Amount* serves as the treatment (T), the protected attributes (Z) are *Age* ($Z1$) and *Personal Status and Gender* ($Z2$), and the outcome (O) is the predicted risk label. This setup allows us to evaluate whether the treatment (*credit amount*) and outcome (*risk*) are influenced by protected variables, and to quantify these effects using ARC's metrics, Weighted Rejection Score (WRS), Deconfounding Impact Estimate (DIE%) (using Propensity Score Matching (PSM) and G-Computation).

4.2.1.2 Test Models

Two predictive models were trained: a linear model (Logistic Regression) and a non-linear ensemble model (Random Forest), along with Random and Biased baseline models. The random baseline produces purely stochastic predictions drawn uniformly from the output range, serving as a lower bound for meaningful performance. The biased baseline, on the other hand, was constructed by systematically skewing the predicted risk values toward one protected group, resulting in higher predicted risk scores for that group irrespective of actual

Table 4.2 Summary of tasks, data attributes, evaluation metrics, AI models, and source references providing implementation details used in the ARC tool

Task	Data	Attributes	Metrics	AI Models	References
Binary Classification	German Credit Dataset [58]	**Treatment**: Credit Amount (low, medium, high); **Protected**: Age, Gender; **Outcome**: Risk (good/bad)	WRS and PIE %	Logistic Regression, Random	[58]
Sentiment Analysis (SAS)	EEC Dataset [99] with emotion word variations and protected attributes (Gender, Race)	**Treatment**: Emotion Word (positive, negative); **Protected**: Gender, Race; **Outcome**: Sentiment.	WRS and PIE %	TextBlob, NRCLex, Biased, Random	[107, 112]
Group Recommendation	Public data from funding agencies (RFPs) and researcher profiles [219]	**Treatment**: Request For Proposals (RFPs) and researcher profiles; **Protected**: Gender; **Outcome**: Goodness Score	WRS	Random Matching (*M0*), String Matching (*M1*), Semantic Matching (*M2*), Boosted Bandit Learning (*M3*)	[149, 150, 198, 219–221]
Time-series Forecasting (TSFM)	Stock prices (Mar 2023–Apr 2024) from *Yahoo! Finance*	**Treatment**: Semantic, Input-specific, and Composite perturbations; **Protected**: Company, Industry; **Outcome**: Residual	WRS, PIE %, and forecasting accuracy metrics	ARIMA, Random, Biased, ViT-num-spec-large (*VNS1*), ViT-num-spec-small (*VNS2*)	[111]

applicant features. Logistic Regression and Random Forest are among the most widely used models in credit scoring applications [4].

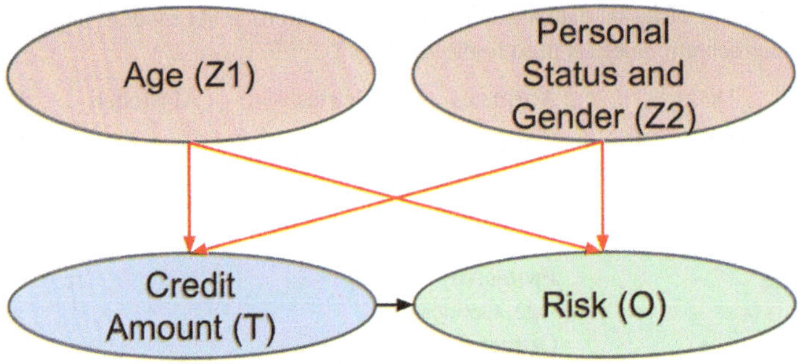

Fig. 4.3 Generalized causal graph for the credit risk classification task. Age ($Z1$) and personal status and gender ($Z2$) represent protected attributes. Arrows from Z to O indicate statistical bias, while additional arrows from Z to T create backdoor paths, leading to confounding effects

Table 4.3 ARC results for the credit risk assessment (Binary Classification) task. Lower WRS, PIE%, and DIE% indicate less bias, while higher Accuracy and F1 indicate better performance

Model	WRS ↓	PIE% ↓	DIE% ↓	Accuracy% ↑	F1 ↑
Random forest	4.6	50.25	13.28	**78**	**0.85**
Logistic regression	1.25	70.82	**1.18**	73	0.83
Random	**0**	**29.87**	4.82	54.50	0.63
Biased	7.15	60.05	6.16	59.50	0.72

4.2.1.3 Test Data

We use the German Credit Dataset [64], which is widely adopted in studies of algorithmic fairness and explainability [131, 224, 233]. The dataset contains 1,000 loan applicant records with 20 attributes, including demographic information (e.g., *age*, *personal status and sex*), financial details (e.g., *credit amount*, *duration*, *checking account status*), and other applicant-related features. These variables are used by banks to assess loan risk. The outcome variable is binary: $Risk \in \{0, 1\}$, where $Risk = 1$ indicates a good credit risk (loan approved) and $Risk = 0$ indicates a bad credit risk (loan rejected).

4.2.1.4 Results

The metric scores or the raw values and ratings obtained from ARC are shown in Tables 4.3 and 4.4 respectively. Among all models, **Random Forest** achieved the highest accuracy (78%) and F1 score (0.85), but this came with moderate bias, indicated by its higher PIE % and DIE% values. **Logistic Regression** performed slightly worse in performance metrics but exhibited lower DIE %, suggesting greater stability once confounding factors were adjusted for. As expected, the **Biased** baseline showed uneven performance across groups, confirming

Table 4.4 Model ratings (1 = best) across ARC metrics for the credit risk assessment task. Lower WRS, PIE%, and DIE% indicate less bias; higher Accuracy and F1 indicate better performance

Model	WRS ↓	PIE% ↓	DIE% ↓	Accuracy% ↑	F1 ↑
Random forest	3	3	3	1	1
Logistic regression	2	4	1	2	2
Random	1	1	2	4	4
Biased	4	2	4	3	3

its intentionally biased behavior, while the **Random** baseline provided low performance but serves as a useful lower bound for comparison. ARC's results show a common trade-off between accuracy and interpretability in credit risk assessment [18]. More complex models tend to fit data better but also amplify bias. By framing these outcomes within a causal structure, ARC helps explain not only how models differ in performance but also *why* those differences arise, translating fairness and instability into measurable, comparable quantities.

Key Insight: Credit Risk Classification

In the binary credit risk classification task, ARC shows how causal analysis can show the accuracy-robustness trade-off. The Random Forest model predicts more accurately overall, but its predictions are also more influenced by protected attributes such as age and gender. Logistic Regression performs slightly worse in accuracy but stays more consistent when these attributes vary.

4.2.2 Case Study 2: Sentiment Analysis

In ARC, we present an illustration of how sentiment analysis systems (SASs) can be rated for bias, while more detailed experiments and evaluations are discussed in our earlier works [107, 112]. In this section, we summarize the key insights from ARC's results. Examining bias in sentiment models remains crucial, as prior studies such as [100] have shown that many SASs display systematic gender and race bias even in simple synthetic texts.

4.2.2.1 Causal Model and Assumptions

The generalized causal graph for this task, shown in Fig. 4.4, represents how protected attributes (*Gender*, *Race*) and the chosen *Emotion Word* influence the output sentiment

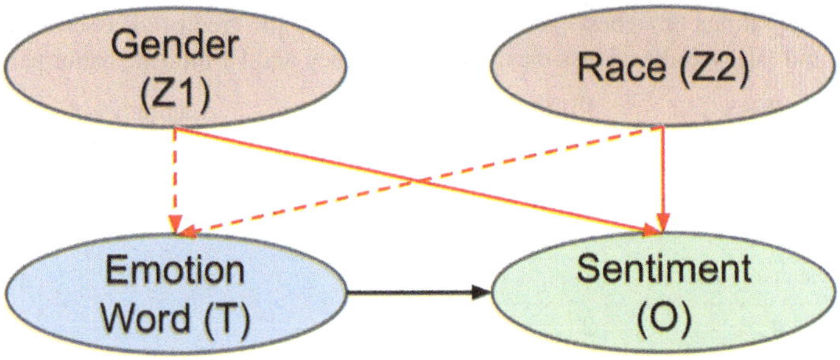

Fig. 4.4 Generalized causal graph for the sentiment analysis task. Gender ($Z1$) and race ($Z2$) represent protected attributes. Solid arrows from Z to O indicate statistical bias, where Z affects O. When dashed arrows from Z to T are also present (as determined by the data), these together with the existing solid arrows create backdoor paths, leading to confounding effects

produced by a SAS. The desired causal pathway is from the *Emotion Word* (T) to the predicted *Sentiment* (O), while paths from protected attributes (Z) to the output ($Z \rightarrow O$) or from the treatment through the protected attribute (backdoor path; $T \leftarrow Z \rightarrow O$) are considered undesirable. ARC quantifies their influence through metrics such as WRS, PIE %, and DIE %.

4.2.2.2 Test Models

In ARC, we evaluated four SASs that represent a diverse range of architectures and behaviors:

- **TextBlob** (S_t): [121] A lexicon-based sentiment analyzer that computes both polarity and subjectivity for a given text. The polarity score lies in the range $[-1, 1]$, with -1 representing negative and $+1$ representing positive sentiment, while subjectivity ranges from 0 (objective) to 1 (subjective). TextBlob uses the *PatternAnalyzer* from the Pattern library, which relies on precompiled word lists and part-of-speech tags to determine sentiment orientation.
- **NRCLex** (S_n): [144] A lexicon-based sentiment analyzer built on the NRC Emotion Lexicon, which measures emotional affect across approximately 27,000 English words. It uses the National Research Council Canada (NRC) affect lexicon and the NLTK WordNet synonym sets to assign scores for basic emotions (e.g., joy, fear, anger, trust) and sentiment polarity. The aggregated polarity score lies in the range $[-1, 1]$.
- **Biased SAS** (S_b): A deliberately biased model that assigns positive sentiment (+1) to sentences containing female gender terms and negative sentiment (-1) to all others, irrespective of emotion words.
- **Random SAS** (S_r): A random baseline that assigns sentiment scores uniformly from $[-1, 1]$, independent of input content.

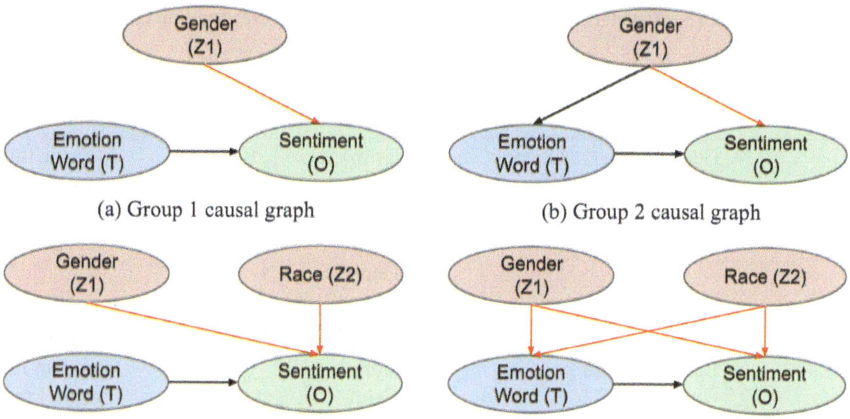

(a) Group 1 causal graph (b) Group 2 causal graph

(c) Group 3 causal graph (d) Group 4 causal graph

Fig. 4.5 Causal graphs for the four dataset groups used in the sentiment analysis task. Each diagram corresponds to a group in Table 4.5

4.2.2.3 Test Data

We used the **Equity Evaluation Corpus (EEC)** [100], which provides controlled sentence templates with variations for gender, race, and emotion words. To examine how such attributes can causally affect sentiment predictions, we generated four dataset groups corresponding to the causal models shown in Fig. 4.5 and summarized in Table 4.5. Each group denotes a different causal relationship between the protected attributes, *Gender* ($Z1$) and *Race* ($Z2$), *Emotion Word* (T), and the output sentiment (O). This design is motivated by the way real-world text data often exhibit imbalances. For example, on social platforms like X (formerly, twitter), emotion words such as "furious" or "grateful" may be associated disproportionately with one gender over another. When such patterns exist in training data, they introduce a causal link from gender ($Z1$) to the emotion word (T). Gender ($Z1$) may also influence the sentiment predicted (O) by a sentiment analysis system (SAS), either directly, if the model learns implicit gender associations, or indirectly, through confounding relationships in the data. To capture and test these possibilities in a controlled setting, we construct four groups of datasets, each representing a distinct setup:

- **Group 1 (Figure** 4.5**a)** Gender ($Z1$) and emotion word (T) are generated independently, i.e., there is no confounding between them. This is the ideal setting, where the sentiment should depend solely on the emotion word ($T \rightarrow O$).
- **Group 2 (Figure** 4.5**b)** Gender ($Z1$) influences the choice of emotion words (T), creating a backdoor path ($T \leftarrow Z \rightarrow O$). Positive emotion words (e.g., *happy*, *glad*) are more frequently paired with one gender, while negative ones (e.g., *grim*, *depressing*) are paired with another, simulating real-world data bias.

Table 4.5 Datasets constructed for the sentiment analysis task, corresponding causal graphs shown in Fig. 4.5

Group	Input	Possible confounders	Choice of emotion words	Causal model (Fig. 4.5)	Example sentences
1	Gender, Emotion Word	None	{Grim}, {Happy}, {Grim, Happy}, {Depressing, Happy, Glad}	Fig. 4.5a	I made this boy feel grim; I made this girl feel grim
2	Gender, Emotion Word	Gender	{Grim, Happy}, {Grim, Depressing, Happy}	Fig. 4.5b	I made this woman feel grim; I made this boy feel happy
3	Gender, Race, Emotion Word	None	{Grim, Happy}, {Depressing, Happy, Glad}	Fig. 4.5c	I made Adam feel happy; I made Alonzo feel happy
4	Gender, Race, Emotion Word	Gender, Race	{Grim, Happy}, {Grim, Depressing, Happy}	Fig. 4.5d	I made Torrance feel grim; Adam feels happy

- **Group 3 (Figure 4.5c)** Both gender ($Z1$) and race ($Z2$) are included but generated independently.
- **Group 4 (Figure 4.5d)** Both gender ($Z1$) and race ($Z2$) jointly influence emotion word assignment, forming two backdoor paths. For instance, positive words are more frequently associated with "European male" and negative words with "African-American female," indicating known disparities reported in prior fairness literature [35].

We used multiple emotion word sets such as E1: {*Grim*}, E2: {*Happy*}, E3: {*Grim, Happy*}, E4: {*Grim, Depressing, Happy*}, and E5: {*Depressing, Happy, Glad*}. In the non-confounded groups (Groups 1 and 3), all five sets (E1-E5) were used to produce diverse datasets. Here, emotion words serve as the treatment variable (T), with combinations containing both positive and negative words (e.g., E3-E5) defining "treated" (positive) and "untreated" (negative) samples for causal effect estimation. In the confounded groups (Groups 2 and 4), the association of emotion words with protected attributes is intentionally varied to simulate data imbalances. These groups primarily use the sets E3-E5 to examine how confounding affects the relationship between emotion word and sentiment before and after deconfounding, as captured by the PIE%. Together, the variation of emotion word

Table 4.6 ARC results for the Sentiment Analysis task across all groups. Lower WRS and PIE% indicate lower statistical and confounding biases respectively

Model	Group 1 WRS ↓	Group 2 PIE% ↓	Group 3 WRS ↓	Group 4 PIE% ↓
TextBlob SAS	0.0	90.0	0.0	90.0
NRCLex SAS	1.2	69.23	0.0	100.0
Random SAS	1.9	42.69	0.6	39.75
Biased SAS	4.6	184.62	4.6	75.0

Table 4.7 Model rankings (1 = best) across ARC metrics for the Sentiment Analysis task. Lower values indicate lower bias and greater robustness

Model	Group 1 WRS ↓	Group 2 PIE% ↓	Group 3 WRS ↓	Group 4 PIE% ↓
TextBlob SAS	1	3	1	3
NRCLex SAS	2	2	1	4
Random SAS	3	1	2	1
Biased SAS	4	4	3	2

sets and their associations with demographic attributes allow testing of both statistical bias (Groups 1 and 3) and confounding bias (Groups 2 and 4).

4.2.2.4 Results

We evaluated four SASs in ARC: **TextBlob-based SAS** (S_t), **NRCLex SAS** (S_n), **Random SAS** (S_r), and **Biased SAS** (S_b), across the four dataset groups introduced earlier. The quantitative results and model ratings are shown in Tables 4.6 and 4.7.

- **Group 1 (No Confounding)**. When gender ($Z1$) and emotion words (T) were generated independently, both TextBlob and NRCLex produced zero and near-zero WRS values respectively, indicating that their sentiment predictions (O) were unaffected by gender. The Random SAS showed some discrepancy, while the Biased SAS exhibited the highest discrepancy.
- **Group 2 (Gender as Confounder)**. As gender ($Z1$) influenced the distribution of emotion words (T), the Biased SAS showed the strongest confounding bias, with PIE% far exceeding the other systems. TextBlob and NRCLex remained stable, demonstrating minimal shifts in sentiment predictions after deconfounding. Random SAS showed moderate PIE%.
- **Group 3 (Gender and Race, Independent)**. With two protected attributes included but generated independently, TextBlob and NRCLex again recorded WRS score of zero when

both gender ($Z1$) and race ($Z2$) were considered as protected attributes (Z) for analysis. The Biased SAS continued to display high bias, consistent with its design.

- **Group 4 (Gender and Race as Joint Confounders)**. When both gender ($Z1$) and race ($Z2$) influenced the distribution of emotion words, the Biased SAS showed the clearest distortion (spurious correlation due to confounding bias) in sentiment predictions (O). TextBlob and NRCLex remained comparatively stable, showing little change in output despite the added confounding. The Random SAS produced moderate inconsistent shifts. Taken together with the Group 2 results, these findings suggest that lexicon-based systems are relatively robust to changes in protected attributes, while deliberately biased or random models amplify such effects.

Tables 4.6 and 4.7 summarize the overall findings. ARC distinguishes intrinsic model bias (as seen in S_b) from bias amplified through data confounding. Since the treatment variable (*emotion word*) is categorical, we report only PIE% values computed using propensity score matching (PSM), which is well-suited for categorical treatments [206]. The results confirm that TextBlob and NRCLex maintain consistently low bias across all experimental conditions, while the Biased SAS amplifies dependencies on protected attributes and the Random SAS behaves inconsistently across metrics. A more extensive evaluation, including GRU-based and transformer-based DistilBERT sentiment analyzers, was presented in our earlier work [112], where the same causal framework was applied at scale to compare deep, lexicon-based, and synthetic AI models.

Key Insight: Sentiment Analysis

ARC shows that lexicon-based models such as TextBlob and NRCLex remain largely stable or fair even when confounding is introduced, whereas biased or random systems show strong shifts in predicted sentiment in the presence of race and gender attributes.

4.2.3 Case Study 3: Group Recommendation

In this case study, we explore ULTRA, a deployed system for matching researchers to funding opportunities [219–221]. ULTRA extracts required skills from proposal calls, extracts researcher expertise profiles, and then constructs teams that attempt to satisfy proposal requirements while maintaining reasonable team size, redundancy, and robustness. In this case study, ARC examines whether these recommendations differ across gender groups when the outcome of interest is the team goodness score produced by ULTRA's models.

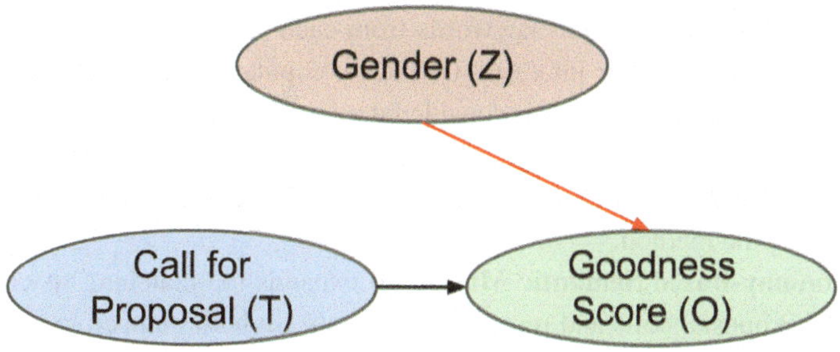

Fig. 4.6 Generalized causal graph for the group recommendation/team formation task. Gender (Z) acts as the protected attribute. Solid arrows from Z to O indicate statistical bias, where Z affects O

4.2.3.1 Causal Model and Assumptions

The causal graph for this task is shown in Fig. 4.6. The protected attribute Z is researcher gender. The treatment T refers to the proposal call selected by the user. Each call has a distinct skill profile and therefore changes the set of researchers that ULTRA considers suitable. The outcome O is the team goodness score produced by ULTRA. The score is a weighted combination of four measurable properties of a candidate team: coverage, redundancy, team size, and k-robustness. Coverage measures the proportion of skills required by the proposal call that are collectively satisfied by the team. Redundancy captures whether multiple members share the same required skills, which can be useful when proposals expect overlapping expertise but can also increase team size unnecessarily. Team size enters the score because larger teams reduce the per-person share of funding and may increase coordination costs, while smaller teams risk failing to meet skill requirements. The final component, k-robustness, tests how well the team continues to satisfy the proposal requirements if up to k members are removed. ULTRA computes each metric on a normalized scale and then applies a set of fixed weights that reward high coverage and robustness and penalize excess redundancy and large team sizes. The weighted values are averaged and normalized to the interval [0, 1], resulting in a single score that captures how well a team meets the proposal requirements under considerations of size and stability.

4.2.3.2 Test Models

ULTRA provides four team formation methods that differ in how they match proposal requirements and researcher expertise, and therefore produce teams with distinct structures. Each method relies on the same pool of proposal calls and researcher profiles but applies a different matching strategy.

- **M0 (Random Matching)** constructs teams by sampling researchers uniformly at random. Apart from ensuring that each team contains at least two members, M0 does not use proposal skills or researcher interests.

- **M1 (String Matching)** extracts keywords from each proposal call and compares them directly with the researcher interests. ULTRA computes string overlaps using a fixed matching threshold. A researcher is considered relevant if the overlap between a proposal skill and the researcher's interest exceeds this threshold. Teams are then constructed by selecting all researchers who meet at least one of the required skills, up to a size cap determined by the method.
- **M2 (Taxonomy-Based Semantic Matching)** expands the matching space beyond literal words. Proposal skills and researcher interests are both mapped to concepts in the ACM Computing Classification System using n-gram similarity. M2 checks whether the mapped concepts fall under the same parent category in the taxonomy. This allows, for example, "natural language processing" and "knowledge representation" to be identified as conceptually related despite having little lexical overlap. Teams are formed by collecting researchers who match either the exact concepts or their immediate ancestors in the taxonomy.
- **M3 (Boosted Bandit Learning)** uses a relational learning approach. ULTRA represents the proposal requirements, researcher skills, and existing team assignments as relational predicates. It then trains a set of boosted regression trees that approximate the conditional probability that a researcher is a suitable candidate for a given proposal. These trees act as rules learned from the data. At recommendation time, the method applies these learned rules to estimate which researchers are most likely to contribute to the proposal and selects the top candidates using a greedy policy. The learned rules capture interactions that are not explicitly encoded in the proposal or skill text, such as common pairings of particular research areas.

Because each model draws on different sources of information and applies different selection mechanisms, they often produce teams of different sizes and compositions. ARC evaluates whether the teams produced by these methods lead to differences in outcomes across gender groups when the team goodness score is used as the outcome for causal analysis.

4.2.3.3 Test Data

The data for this task are adapted from the ULTRA system, which collects publicly available proposal calls and researcher profiles [219]. Proposal calls contain textual descriptions of required skills, and researcher profiles include research interests obtained from faculty webpages and Google Scholar. ULTRA processes these texts to extract skill-related terms that can be matched by its four team construction methods. The system then forms candidate teams for each proposal using M0 through M3 and computes a goodness score for every team based on coverage, redundancy, team size, and k-robustness. ARC uses the goodness scores produced by the ULTRA models as the outcome variable and compares these values across gender groups to assess statistical differences.

4.2.3.4 Experimental Setup and Results

ARC was run with Gender as the protected attribute and WRS as the evaluation metric. WRS tests whether the distributions of goodness scores differ across gender groups. The partial order of WRS values is shown below:

$$M0 = 0.0, \quad M1 = 0.0, \quad M2 = 2.3, \quad M3 = 0.0.$$

The resulting ARC ratings were:

$$\{M0 : 1, \ M1 : 1, \ M3 : 1, \ M2 : 2\}.$$

M0, M1, and M3 all have WRS values of 0.0, which indicates that their goodness scores do not show measurable differences across gender groups in the current dataset. M2 (semantic matching) is the only method with a nonzero WRS. This is consistent with how it uses the ACM Computing Classification System. Unlike the string-based methods, M2 does not rely only on exact keyword overlap. It maps proposal topics and researcher interests into higher-level ACM categories and treats researchers as relevant if they fall anywhere within those categories. If one gender is more common in certain ACM categories in the dataset, this broader matching can pull in more researchers from that group for specific proposal types. As a result, the teams produced by M2 can differ across gender simply because the semantic categories themselves are unevenly populated, which explains the observed disparity in goodness scores. Under these treatment and data conditions, M2 is therefore the only model that shows statistical differences across gender groups, while the other methods do not.

Key Insight: Group Recommendation

ARC shows that the taxonomy-based semantic matching method (M2) is the only model that shows statistical bias across gender groups, while the other methods do not.

4.2.4 Case Study 4: Time-Series Forecasting

This case study applies ARC to time-series forecasting models that predict daily stock prices. The goal is to examine how different input perturbations and confounders influence the models' residual errors (the difference between models' predictions and ground truth at each time step in each time-series) when the task is carried out in a black-box setting.

4.2.4.1 Causal Model and Assumptions

The causal graph for this task is shown in Fig. 4.7. Company ($Z1$) and Industry ($Z2$) act as protected attributes, collectively denoted as Z. Although Z is not provided as an explicit input to the model, stock prices associated with different companies and industries may act as proxies for these attributes. For example, technology companies often have stock prices in a higher range compared to pharmaceutical companies.

The directed edge $Z \rightarrow O$ represents the direct effect of the protected attribute on the outcome, where O denotes the maximum forecasting residual over the prediction horizon. Concretely, for each forecasting window, residuals are computed at every predicted timestep, and O corresponds to the largest deviation between the predicted and true values within that window. We refer to this quantity as the maximum residual (or forecasting error). This choice represents the worst-case forecasting error rather than average behavior and is discussed in detail in Sect. 4.2.4.4. This effect is measured as *statistical bias*, corresponding to how forecast errors differ systematically across values of Z.

The treatment variable T represents the type of input perturbation applied to the time series, including the unperturbed case. These perturbations are described in detail in Sect. 4.2.4.4. The edge $T \rightarrow O$ represents the causal effect of perturbations on the model's residuals and is central to evaluating model robustness.

In some data distributions, for example for certain companies or industries, the probability of applying a perturbation (T) may depend on the protected attributes (Z), giving rise to the edge $Z \rightarrow T$ (e.g., some companies might have data that is more noisy than other companies' stock prices). When this edge is present, Z acts as a confounder and opens a backdoor path $T \leftarrow Z \rightarrow O$, introducing a spurious association between T and O. In such cases, the causal effect of perturbations must be estimated using the distribution $P(O \mid do(T))$ by adjusting for Z.

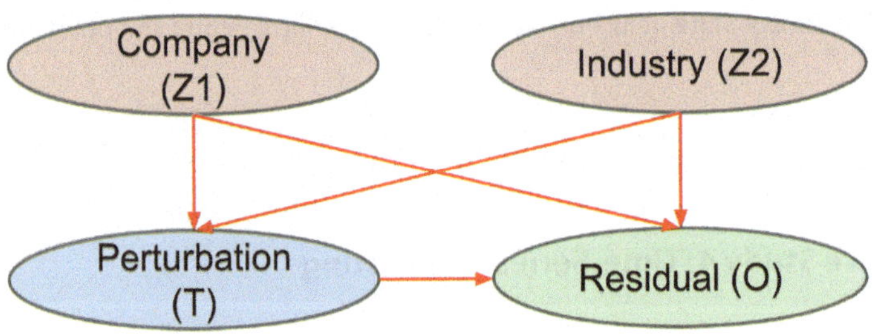

Fig. 4.7 Generalized causal graph for the time-series forecasting task. Industry ($Z1$) and Company ($Z2$) represent the protected attributes. Arrows from Z to O indicate statistical bias. The structure $T \leftarrow Z \rightarrow O$ forms the backdoor path between the perturbation (T) and the residual (O)

Table 4.8 Overview of the architectural details of test models. *Best guess in the absence of official information

Model	Mode	Size	Purpose & Arch.	Inf. Time (sec/sample)
Gemini 1.5 Flash	Multi	32B*	GP-1A, 1B, Decoder	1.6 (1A); 10.2 (1B)
Phi-3-vision	Multi	4.2B	GP-2A, 2B, Enc-Dec	19.7 (1A); 26.6 (1B)
MOMENT-large	Uni	385M	TS-1, Encoder	0.315
Chronos-T5-small	Uni	46M	TS-2, Enc-Dec	0.811
ViT-num-spec	Multi	86M	TS-3, Encoder	6

4.2.4.2 Test Models

In [110, 111], we evaluated six foundation models (FMs) and three baseline models. Among the FMs, four are used directly, while two (Gemini-V and Phi-3) have both uni-modal and multi-modal variants, making them distinct models. Table 4.8 provides an overview of the FM architectures. We also consider two ViT-num-spec models, which are vision transformer-based models trained for time-series forecasting task.

Foundation Models

1. **MOMENT** (S_m) [73] is an open-source FM for forecasting, classification, anomaly detection, and imputation in zero-shot and few-shot settings. It is based on the T5-Large encoder [170] and can be fine-tuned if needed.
2. **Chronos** (S_c) [12] is a pretrained probabilistic time-series model that tokenizes time-series values using scaling and quantization. It employs a T5 encoder-decoder and is trained via cross-entropy loss. We use Chronos-T5-Small.
3. **Gemini-V** (S_g, S_g^{ni}) [213] is a multi-modal FM designed to process both text and images. We use S_g (numeric-only mode) that processes only numerical time-series data, and S_g^{ni} (numeric + vision mode) that processes numerical data and time-series line plots.
4. **Phi-3** (S_p, S_p^{ni}) [1] is a lightweight, state-of-the-art multi-modal FM. We use S_p (numeric-only mode) that processes only numerical time-series data, and S_p^{ni} (numeric + vision mode) that processes numerical data and time-series line plots. Below is the prompt template used for time-series forecasting with Gemini-V and Phi-3 models (text highlighted in red is omitted for uni-modal forecasting):

Prompt to Uni-modal and Multi-modal FMs

"You are a time series forecasting model that only outputs the forecasted numerical values." "***Input***: `<time series>`" *"Given the input time series for the past 80 time steps and the corresponding time series plot, can you forecast the next 20 time steps? Provide a list of 20 numeric values only. Do not provide any discussion."*

Prompt to Multi-modal FMs for P6

"You are a time series forecasting model that only outputs the forecasted numerical values." "***Input***: `<time series>`" *"Given the input time series from the past 80 time steps and the corresponding sentiment intensity plot, where darker shades indicate more negative sentiment and lighter shades indicate more positive sentiment, Provide a list of 20 numeric values only. Do not provide any discussion."*

5. **ViT-num-spec Models** (S_{v1}, S_{v2}): We employ the **ViT-num-spec** model [234], which combines a **vi**sion **t**ransformer with a multimodal time-frequency **spec**tro-gram, augmented by the intensities of **num**eric time series for time series forecasting. This model improves predictive accuracy by leveraging both visual and numerical data. Specifically, it transforms numeric time series into images using a time-frequency spectrogram and utilizes a vision transformer (ViT) encoder with a multilayer perceptron (MLP) head for future predictions.
Time-Frequency Spectrogram: Building on the method of [234], we use wavelet transforms [50] to create time-frequency spectrograms from time series data. Specifically, we employ the Morlet wavelet [185] with scale s and central frequency $\omega_0 = 5$, as detailed in Eq. 4.1:

$$\psi(x) = \sqrt{\frac{1}{s}}\pi^{-\frac{1}{4}} \exp\left(-\frac{x^2}{2s^2}\right) \exp\left(j\omega_0 \frac{x}{s}\right) \tag{4.1}$$

This method convolves the time series with wavelets at various scales, producing coefficients that indicate signal strength at different frequencies. These magnitudes are visualized in a spectrogram, with higher frequencies at the top and lower ones at the bottom. To retain sign information, a stripe from the standardized numeric time series is added to the top of the spectrogram image. This enhanced image is then used as input for the vision transformer model.

Vision Transformer: In the next stage, the ViT-num-spec uses a vision transformer with an MLP head for time series forecasting. Input images are segmented into 16 × 16 non-overlapping patches, projected into tokens, and augmented with 1D positional embeddings. The encoder converts these patches into latent representations. For our implementation, 128 × 128 images have price movements in a 16 × 128 top row, with the spectrogram occupying the remaining 112 × 128 space below.
We trained two variations of the ViT-num-spec model using two real-world datasets and conducted evaluations using a separate dataset. S_{v1} (Pre-COVID training) was trained on S&P 500 stock data from 2000–2014 (46,875 training samples, 46,857 validation samples). S_{v2} (COVID-period training) was trained on data from March 2020-November 2022 (7,478 training samples, 7,475 validation samples).

Baselines

We consider the following baselines:

1. **Auto Regressive Integrated Moving Average (ARIMA)** (S_a) is a widely used statistical approach for time series forecasting. It combines three different components: Autoregressive (AR), differencing (I), and moving average (MA) to capture the patterns in the time-series data and predict the next 20 values.
2. **Biased system** (S_b) is an extreme baseline biased towards META and GOOG (technology companies), assigning residuals of 0 and 200 respectively, while assigning higher residuals to other companies, representing maximum bias.
3. **Random system** (S_r) assigns random price predictions within a company range for contextually meaningful values.

4.2.4.3 Test Data

The experiments are conducted using daily stock price data collected from Yahoo! Finance for six publicly traded companies spanning three industries. The selected companies are Meta (META) and Google (GOOG) from the technology sector, Pfizer (PFE) and Merck (MRK) from the pharmaceutical sector, and Wells Fargo (WFC) and Citigroup (C) from the financial services sector. The dataset covers the period from March 28, 2023, to April 22, 2024. For each company, we use a sliding window of 80 consecutive trading days as input to predict the subsequent 20 trading days. To separate training and evaluation, stock prices from March 28, 2023, to March 22, 2024, are used to construct input windows, while the forecasts are evaluated against the realized prices from March 23, 2024, to April 22, 2024. This dataset design supports analysis at multiple levels: comparisons across companies within the same industry, comparisons across industries with different price ranges and the volatility in prices, and assessment of how input perturbations affect forecasting errors.

4.2.4.4 Experimental Setup and Results

Perturbations To evaluate robustness under different adversarial conditions, we apply six perturbations to the input time series containing 80 stock prices. These perturbations represent common sources of error in AI models built for finance applications as well as modality-specific vulnerabilities in multimodal models. We group them into semantic, syntactic, input-specific, and composite perturbations.

Semantic perturbations Semantic perturbations alter the numerical values of the time series in a way that changes their meaning while preserving the overall structure of the data.

- **P1: Drop-to-zero**. Every 80-th value in the input time series is replaced with zero. This perturbation simulates data entry errors or missing sensor readings that are incorrectly encoded as zero values. Because a sliding window of size n is used to construct inputs, each window contains at least one zero-valued entry.
- **P2: Value-halved**. Every 80-th value in the input time series is reduced to half of its original magnitude. This perturbation represents numerical distortions, such as unit conversion errors or periodic price adjustments, and introduces a subtler semantic shift than P1 while still affecting the scale of the series.

Syntactic perturbation Syntactic perturbations affect the structure or completeness of the data without directly modifying its semantic content.

- **P3: Missing values.** Every 80-th value in the input time series is replaced with a null value. This perturbation models incomplete data records caused by transmission failures or data collection gaps. Models must either handle missing values explicitly or rely on implicit imputation mechanisms.

Input-specific perturbations Input-specific perturbations target the visual components of multimodal inputs and are applicable only to models that consume image data.

- **P4: Single pixel change**. A single pixel at a fixed location in each visual input (the center of the time-frequency spectrogram or line plot) is altered to black. This perturbation is inspired by prior work demonstrating that localized pixel-level changes can disproportionately affect vision-based models, despite minimal visual distortion [207].
- **P5: Saturation change**. In [238], the authors showed that the adversarial perturbations in the S-channel (or saturation channel) of an image in HSV (Hue Saturation Value) form ensures a high success rate for attacks compared to other channels. In our work, we increase the saturation of the multi-modal input ten-fold based on the intuition that a subtle change can affect the models' predictions.

Composite perturbation The final perturbation evaluates robustness when the forecasting model is composed with an auxiliary AI system, a sentiment analysis system (SAS).

- **P6: Sentiment-based composite perturbation.** We consider a composite case where forecasting model is combined with SAS to represent the influence of market sentiment on stock prediction [142]. We assess sentiment for each time series by passing the corresponding time-series line plot to a zero-shot CLIP-based SAS [33, 168], which outputs sentiment intensity values (negative (−1), neutral (0), positive (1)). These labels are scaled to [0, 255] and represented as a sentiment intensity stripe. This zero-shot CLIP-based SAS may exhibit bias or inaccuracies; the goal is to study the robustness of forecasting model in conjunction with such an AI model.

Together, these six perturbations span a range of realistic failures, from coarse numerical perturbation to subtle visual perturbations and cross-model error propagation. This diversity enables a comprehensive evaluation of robustness across both uni-modal and multi-modal time-series forecasting models.

Forecasting Accuracy Metrics In addition to measuring statistical bias (WRS), confounding bias (PIE %), and perturbation impact (ATE), ARC also measures forecasting accuracy, using the following metrics [128]:

Symmetric mean absolute percentage error (SMAPE) measures the relative difference between predicted and actual values and assigns equal weight to over- and under-estimations. It is defined as,

$$SMAPE = \frac{1}{T}\sum_{t=1}^{T}\frac{|x_t - \hat{x}_t|}{(|x_t| + |\hat{x}_t|)/2}, \tag{4.2}$$

where $T = 20$ is the total number of observations in the predicted time series. SMAPE scores range from 0 to 2, with lower scores indicating more precise forecasts.

Mean absolute scaled error (MASE) measures the mean absolute error of forecasts relative to that of a naive one-step forecast on the training data.

$$MASE = \frac{\frac{1}{T}\sum_{i=t+1}^{t+T}|x_i - \hat{x}_i|}{\frac{1}{t}\sum_{i=1}^{t}|x_i - x_{i-1}|}, \tag{4.3}$$

where in our case, $t = 80$, and $T = 100$. Lower MASE values indicate better forecasts.

Sign Accuracy quantifies the proportion of correctly predicted directional changes in the time series. A higher accuracy indicates better alignment with actual trend movements.

$$\text{Sign Accuracy} = \frac{1}{T}\sum_{t=1}^{T} 1\left(\text{sign}(\hat{x}_t - \hat{x}_{t-1}) = \text{sign}(x_t - x_{t-1})\right), \tag{4.4}$$

where T is the total number of predicted time steps, x_t is the actual value, and $\hat{x}_t$ is the predicted value at time t. The indicator function $1(\cdot)$ returns 1 if the predicted sign matches the actual sign and 0 otherwise. Higher Sign Accuracy values indicate better directional prediction.

Results

Table 4.9 summarizes the empirical findings across all four research questions by reporting average metric values across models and perturbations.

RQ1: Effect of protected attributes (Z) on forecasting errors (O).

Statistical bias persists even when perturbations are applied uniformly across all samples (i.e., when there is no causal link from Z to T). Using WRS, the ARIMA baseline (S_a) exhibits the lowest statistical bias (3.96), while the Phi-3 numeric model (S_p) exhibits the highest (6.27). Across perturbations, the unperturbed setting (P0) leads to the highest average bias (5.70). Inter-industry comparisons consistently exhibit larger discrepancies than intra-industry comparisons, establishing industry ($Z2$) as a stronger source of statistical bias than company.

RQ2: Confounding effect of protected attributes (Z) on the relationship between perturbations (T) and forecasting errors (O) impact.

When perturbation assignment depends on protected attributes, confounding substantially alters the observed relationship between perturbations (T) and forecasting errors (O). As reported in Table 4.9, the Gemini-V multimodal model (S_g^{ni}) shows the lowest confounding bias (PIE% $=$ 1107.66), whereas the Phi-3 multimodal model (S_p^{ni}) shows the highest (2778.06). Among perturbations, P5 produces the largest confounding bias (3646.20). Across all models, industry induces higher confounding bias than company.

RQ3: Causal impact of perturbations on forecasting errors. Table 4.9 shows that S_g^{ni} has the lowest average treatment effect (ATE $=$ 5.89), while S_a has the highest (27.73). Among perturbations, P3 has the smallest causal impact (ATE $=$ 9.96), whereas P1 has the largest (20.25). Industry ($Z2$) again emerges as the confounder that most amplifies perturbation effects.

RQ4: Impact of perturbations on forecasting accuracy.

Accuracy-based results in Table 4.9 show that Chronos (S_c) achieves the best overall accuracy (SMAPE $=$ 0.051, MASE $=$ 4.67), while MOMENT (S_m) performs worst among foundation models. Across perturbations, the composite perturbation P6 leads to the largest degradation in SMAPE (0.39) and MASE (176.43), while P1 causes the largest drop in sign accuracy (49.86).

Table 4.9 Summary of the research questions answered in the paper, causal diagram, metrics used in the experiment, average of the metric values compared across different systems (S), average computed across different perturbations (T), and the key conclusions drawn from the experiments

Research question	Metrics used	Comparison across systems	Comparison across perturbations	Key conclusions
RQ1: To what extent does Z affect O?	WRS	$\{S_a$: 3.96, S_g: 5.05, S_r: 5.15, S_{v2}: 5.20, S_g^{ni}: 5.44, S_c: 5.46, S_p^{ni}: 5.48, S_{v1}: 5.71, S_m: 5.75, S_p: 6.27, S_b: 6.9$\}$	{P4: 5.42, P1: 5.49, P3: 5.51, P5: 5.52, P6: 5.52, P2: 5.55, P0: 5.70}	**S with low statistical bias**: S_a. **S with high statistical bias**: S_p. **T that led to more statistical bias**: P0 **Analysis with more discrepancy**: Inter-industry
RQ2: To what extent does Z affect the relationship between P and O, when Z also affects T?	PIE %	$\{S_g^{ni}$: 1107.66, S_g: 1115.08, S_{v2}: 1346.46, S_a: 1448.29, S_{v1}: 1848.20, S_p: 2459.30, S_m: 2544.20, S_r: 2668.52, S_c: 2755.50, S_p^{ni}: 2778.06, S_b: 4758.16$\}$	{P1: 1711.88, P4: 2035.95, P3: 2057.31, P6: 2410.28, P2: 2628.52, P5: 3646.20}	**S with low confounding bias**: S_g^{ni}. **S with high confounding bias**: S_p^{ni}. **T that led to more confounding bias**: P5. **Confounder that led to more bias**: *Industry*
RQ3: Does T affect O when Z may have an effect on O?	ATE	$\{S_g^{ni}$: 5.89, S_{v1}: 7.34, S_c: 7.80, S_m: 9.83, S_g: 6.46, S_{v1}: 6.46, S_p^{ni}: 12.66, S_p: 15.98, S_r: 21.57, S_a: 27.73, S_b: 33.95$\}$	{P3: 9.96, P6: 12.2, P2: 12.9, P4: 13.19, P5: 18.36, P1: 20.25}	**S with low ATE**: S_g^{ni}. **S with high ATE**: S_a. **T with low ATE**: P3. **T with high ATE**: P1. **Confounder that led to high ATE**: *Industry*
RQ4: Does T affect the accuracy of S?	SMAPE, MASE, Sign Accuracy	**SMAPE**: $\{S_c$: 0.051, S_{v1}: 0.053, S_g: 0.055, S_a: 0.058, S_{v2}: 0.06, S_g^{ni}: 0.06, S_r: 0.83, S_p^{ni}: 0.084, S_p: 0.097, S_m: 0.098, S_b: 1.276$\}$; **MASE**: $\{S_c$: 4.67, S_{v1}: 4.80, S_g: 5.04, S_{v2}: 5.49, S_g^{ni}: 5.76, S_a: 8.54, S_p^{ni}: 7.60, S_p: 9.02, S_m: 9.13, S_r: 86.76, S_b: 947.56 $\}$; **Sign Accuracy**: $\{S_m$: 40.91, S_p: 44.42, S_p^{ni}: 45.24, S_{v2}: 49.33, S_r: 49.75, S_g: 50.93, S_{v1}: 51.34, S_g^{ni}: 51.37, S_c: 51.99, S_a: 58.57, S_b: 62.6$\}$	**SMAPE**: {P0: 0.24, P2: 0.25, P1: 0.26, P3: 0.28, P4: 0.38, P5: 0.38, P6: 0.39}; **MASE**: {P0: 99.06, P2: 99.57, P1: 101.27, P3: 119.66, P4: 175.56, P5: 175.56, P6: 176.43}; **Sign Accuracy**: {P1: 49.86, P0: 51.35, P2: 51, P3: 51.16, P4: 51.79, P5: 51.43, P6: 50};	**S with good performance**: S_c. **S with poor performance**: S_m. **T with high impact on performance**: P6.

Key Insight: Time-Series Forecasting

Taken together, ARC shows that statistical bias, confounding bias, and impact of perturbations capture distinct aspects of model behavior. Industry ($Z2$) consistently dominates company ($Z1$) as a source of bias and confounding. Multimodal foundation models exhibit stronger robustness after deconfounding (ATE), even when they do not achieve the best raw accuracy. The statistical model ARIMA exhibits the lowest level of statistical bias (WRS), while S_g^{ni} exhibits the lowest level of confounding bias (PIE %), and S_c achieves the highest forecasting accuracy.

4.3 How to Use ARC Tool for Custom Tasks?

ARC was designed so that users are not limited to the four example tasks included in the tool. A custom task can be evaluated as long as the user provides three elements: a treatment variable (T), an outcome variable (O), and at least one protected attribute (Z). This section describes how a new task is incorporated into ARC and the practical steps needed to prepare data for analysis.

- **Dataset Selection (Fig.** 4.8**b)**: ARC relies on model predictions under different treatment conditions. To use ARC for a new task, the user assembles a dataset where each row corresponds to a model evaluation instance. The dataset must include the treatment assignment (T), protected attributes (Z), and the resulting outcome (O). When comparing multiple models, each model produces a separate set of outcomes. The protected attribute must be categorical so that ARC can run its hypothesis tests across the groups.
- **Attribute Selection (Fig.** 4.8**c)**: A user has to select a treatment (T) variable in the data. In previous demonstrations, the treatment has represented credit amount, emotion words, proposal calls, or time-series perturbations. For a custom task, the treatment can be any controlled input variation that the user wishes to examine. The outcome (O) is the model output or a transformed version of it. For example, a user who is testing a classifier may use predicted probabilities, while someone studying a forecasting model may use absolute errors. The protected attribute (Z) is chosen from demographic or sensitive variables in the dataset, such as gender, age, or location, depending on the task. ARC expects the dataset provided by the user to have outcomes or predictions from different models they would like to assess.
- **Metric Selection (Fig.** 4.8**d)**: After the dataset is uploaded, ARC prompts the user to select metrics. WRS determines whether the protected attribute affects the outcome distribution. PIE% and DIE% measure confounding by comparing observed and deconfounded

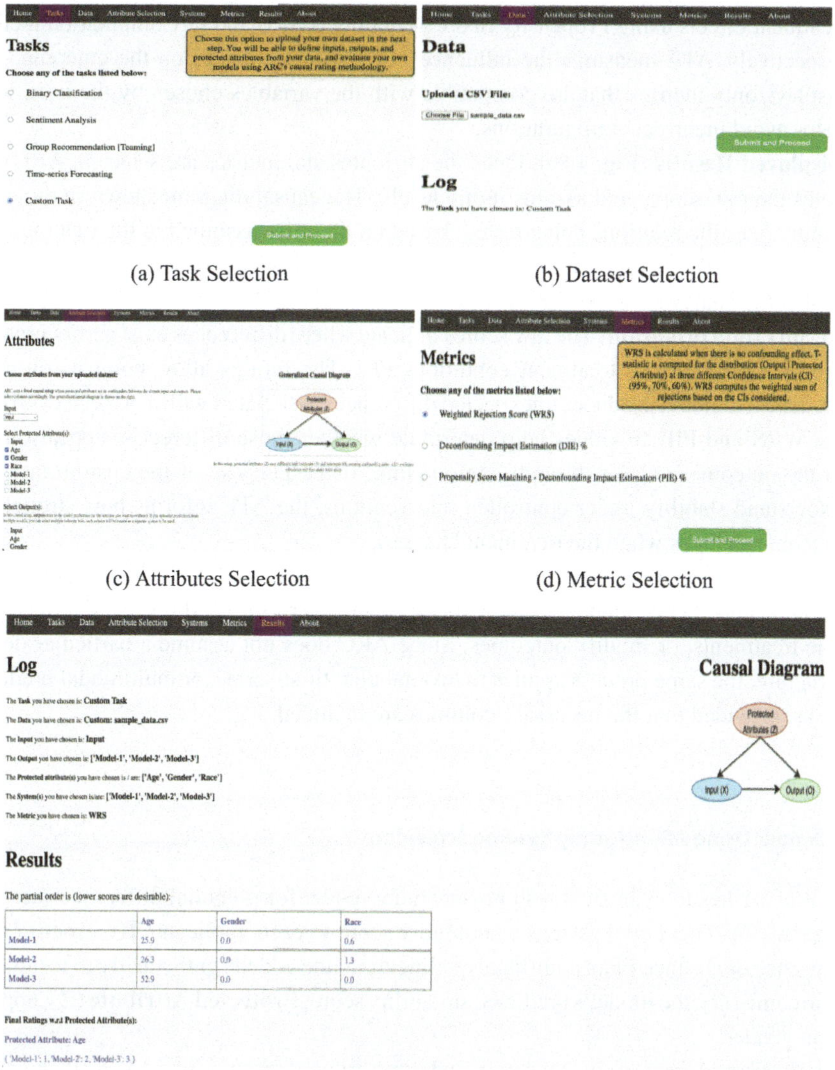

(a) Task Selection (b) Dataset Selection

(c) Attributes Selection (d) Metric Selection

(e) Displayed Results

Fig. 4.8 Step-by-step workflow of the ARC tool, illustrating task setup, dataset upload, attribute and model selection, metric choice, and results visualization

treatment effects using Propensity Score Matching (PSM) and G-Computation methods respectively. ATE measures the influence of treatment changes on the outcome. ARC displays only metrics that are compatible with the variables chosen by the user, which helps avoid incorrect configurations.

- **Displayed Results (Fig.** 4.8**e)**: Once the attributes and metrics are selected, ARC computes the raw scores and assigns rating levels. The causal diagram shown in the output summarizes the relations being tested, based on the roles assigned to the treatment (T), protected attributes (Z), and outcome (O). The results page also logs the user's choices so that the analysis can be reproduced.
- **Results Interpretation**: The raw scores indicate where differences exist across protected groups (Z) or across treatment conditions (T). The ratings allow comparison across models. If a model produces unexpected differences associated with a protected attribute, the WRS and PIE % values help determine whether those differences appear directly in the outcomes (O) or through confounding. If the purpose of the custom task is to understand stability under controlled interventions, the ATE informs how strongly the outcome changes when the treatment changes.
- **Iterating on the task**: It is common for users to adjust their task after examining the initial results. ARC supports this by allowing the user to upload revised datasets, redefine treatments, or modify outcomes. Since ARC does not assume a particular domain structure, the same process applies to text, tabular, time-series, or multimodal prediction tasks, provided that the necessary columns are included.

Example: Using ARC to Study Resume Screening

A user wishes to evaluate a resume-screening model for potential differences across gender (Z). The model assigns a suitability score to each applicant. **Treatment** (T): presence or absence of an additional qualification line added synthetically to resumes. **Outcome** (O): the model's predicted suitability score. **Protected Attribute** (Z): applicant gender.

The user prepares a dataset that includes the original resumes (e.g., $T = 0$), the perturbed resumes (e.g., $T = 1$)), the gender of each applicant (Z), and the corresponding model scores (O). After uploading the data to ARC, the user selects WRS and DIE% to test both statistical differences and confounding. ARC produces raw scores and ratings that show whether the model responds differently to the added qualification across gender groups. This allows the user to see whether the model treats the same perturbation consistently across groups and whether any observed difference is due to confounding between gender and other resume attributes.

4.4 Historical Notes: Evolution of Robustness Assessment Tools

AI Fairness 360 (AIF360) [22] developed by IBM research, represents one of the first concerted efforts to transition fairness research from algorithms to an industrial framework. It has over 71 bias detection metrics such as statistical parity difference, equalized odds difference, generalized entropy index, ...It also has bias mitigation algorithms at various stages of an AI pipeline: pre-processing (e.g., reweighing), in-processing (e.g., adversarial debiasing), and post-processing (e.g., equalized odds). However, it does not support multi-modality and hard to integrate it into continuous deployment pipelines (MLOps). Fairlearn [30], another fairness assessment framework, focuses heavily on *disaggregated evaluation* and the ability to wrap existing estimators. It integrated natively with well-known data science libraries like pandas and scikit-learn. It also provides *meta-algorithms* such as ExponentiatedGradient and GridSearch that iteratively retrain the undelying model with re-weighted data to satisfy fairness constraints like equalized odds and demographic parity while optimizing for accuracy. It also includes adversarial mitigation methods such as AdversarialFairnessClassifier, which brings mitigation capabilities to deep learning frameworks like PyTorch and Tensorflow. However, it does not purport to address representation harms or broader issues of justice. FairGround corpus [194] is not a model evaluation tool per se, but an evaluation infrastructure containing 44 tabular datasets, each annotated with metadata suitable for fairness analysis. The accompanying python package standardizes dataset loading, preprocessing, and splitting. This is critical because recent research has shown minor variations in data preprocessing can drastically alter the results of fairness assessments [194]. Like AIF360 and Fairlearn, FairGround is currently limited to tabular classification tasks, leaving a gap for standardized fairness datasets in vision and NLP.

As limitations of statistical metrics became clear, a new paradigm emerged: behavioral testing. Inspired by software engineering (specifically unit testing and fuzzing), there tools treat AI models as *black-boxes* to be probed with specific inputs to verify expected behaviors. CheckList [174] implements evaluation through a matrix of linguistic capabilities (e.g., Named Entity Recognition (NER)) and test types (e.g., Minimum Functionality Tests (MFT)). It also provides test methods such as Invariance Tests (INV) that tests whether system outcome changes when perturbations are applied to the input. CheckList also provides abstractions (templates like "I {Negation} like {Entity}") and lexicons (using models like RoBERTa) to generate thousands of test cases automatically. However, CheckList is purely behavioral, it cannot explain why a model failed. Google's What-If tool (WIT) addresses the need for non-programmatic auditing. WIT allows users to slice datasets by combinations of features (e.g., Race and Gender) to visualize performance disparities. This is critical for identifying "fairness gerrymandering," where bias is hidden in broad groups but visible in intersections. Because WIT processes data in-browser, it cannot handle massive datasets efficiently.

Adversarial robustness assesses whether models perform accurately under adversarial attacks or perturbations. CleverHans [159] defined the standard for adversarial benchmarking. It provides reference implementations of foundational gradient-based attacks, including Fast Gradient Sign Method (FGSM), Projected Gradient Descent (PGD), and Carlini & Wagner (C&W). However, CleverHans struggled to keep up with the explosion of new attacks and framework shifts (TF1 to TF2/PyTorch). IBM's Adversarial Robustness Toolbox (ART) [155] is the most comprehensive library in adversarial machine learning domain, covering four distinctive threats: evasion (from standard attacks), poisoning (tests if training data has been corrupted), extraction (whether a model can be *stolen* by querying it repeatedly), and privacy issues (e.g., data leakage). However, running a full ART audit, especially with adversarial training or poisoning detection, is computationally prohibitive for large models. TextAttack [145] addresses the issue that NLP attacks were often disjointed. It introduces a system for generating textual adversarial examples. These attacks are built from a goal function (what to achieve), constraints (semantic rules), transformation (how to swap words), and search method (greedy/beam search). Recent developments include, AdvSecureNet [37], which addresses the lack of multi-GPU support and configuration management in older libraries like ART and CleverHans. Another framework, Confidential-PROFITT [187], targets the intersection of privacy and fairness, providing benchmarks for zero-knowledge proofs in fair decision tree training, expanding assessment into the area of cryptographic verification.

Several works have assessed and rated AI systems for trustworthiness from a third-party perspective, explicitly assuming no access to training data or model internals. Reference [200] introduced an early rating framework for AI services based on a two-step testing procedure that probes system behavior under controlled unbiased and biased input distributions, assigning ratings that distinguish whether bias is introduced by the model, propagated from the data, or compensated by the system. The approach was instantiated and empirically evaluated in the context of machine translation and was shown to admit compositional reasoning when AI services are chained together. Follow-on work focused on making these ratings intelligible to non-expert users through visual encodings [27] and demonstrated, via user studies, that the presence and presentation of bias ratings measurably influence trust and service selection decisions [25]. The same rating philosophy was subsequently extended to other black-box AI services, including personalized chatbots [204], where multiple trust-related issues (e.g., bias, abusive language, information leakage, dialog complexity) were aggregated into user-profile-dependent ratings, and search engines in the GLAM domain [214], where the two-step test was adapted to disentangle content bias from interface bias arising from ranking mechanisms, metadata sparsity, and learned semantic associations. While these approaches provide assessments of observable AI behavior and scale across domains, they rely primarily on distributional comparisons, and do not explicitly model the causal effects of protected attributes on system outputs.

The most significant recent shift in AI evaluation is the move from associational metrics (which measure correlation) to causal metrics. Microsoft's DoWhy framework [189] reframes evaluation as a causal inference problem. The authors argue that "no causes in, no causes out", evaluation is impossible without explicit assumptions. It encodes assumptions in a causal graph (DAG), uses graph theory to see if different effects are estimable, calculates effects using methods like PSM, and tests the robustness of the estimate (process is called refutation) it produced by simulating violations (e.g., "Placebo Treatment Refuter"). DoWhy-GCM [31] is an extension of DoWhy that allows for root cause analysis and outlier detection by modeling the generative mechanisms of the data. However, DoWhy's results are only as good as the user-provided causal graph. If the user omits a latent confounder in the graph, DoWhy may proceed with a biased estimate (though the refutation step attempts to handle this). Reference [166] introduces the CausalFairnessInAction library for causal fairness. It decomposes a metric like statistical disparity into three causal components: direct effect (DE), indirect effect (IE), and spurious effect (SE). It also allows counterfactual fairness estimation by calculating whether a specific individual would have received a different outcome had their protected attribute been different, holding all else constant. However, many causal fairness quantities are mathematically unidentifiable from observational data along. They require strong parametric assumptions or access to experimental data, which is rarely available in AI auditing contexts. A recent work, [61], uses causal sensitivity analysis to show that standard fairness metrics are extremely sensitive to bias measurement. A small amount of noise in the *ground truth* labels or unobserved confounding can render fairness assessments vacuously wide and essentially meaningless. CausalBench [226] provides a benchmark based on large-scale biological data. It serves as a rigorous testbed for causal discovery algorithms. References [108, 199] introduced the idea of rating AI models for bias through causal analysis. Reference [112] used this approach to rate sentiment analysis systems for bias and also extended it to assess their impact when used with translators [107]. This causality-based method was also used to rate multi-modal time-series forecasting models for robustness [111]. ARC was built on these causality-based rating methods and provides a general framework and tool to assess AI models for robustness using causally-grounded experimental setups [114].

Causal analysis offers advantages over statistical analysis by determining accountability, aligning with humanistic values, and quantifying the direct influence of various attributes on model performance.

4.5 Chapter Summary

This chapter demonstrates how causality-based rating method can be used across heterogeneous AI tasks, showing that robustness and performance trade-offs can be measured, compared, and interpreted within a single, unified framework.

- ARC re-frames robustness as a *multi-dimensional property* of an AI model, not a single score, separating statistical bias, confounding bias, and treatment impact within a unified setup.

- A fixed causal template (Z, T, O) is shown to be flexible enough to cover tabular, text, recommendation, and time-series tasks without task-specific redesign.
- Baseline models (random and biased) play a critical role, contextualizing ratings and allowing better interpretation of raw metric values.
- In credit risk classification, higher predictive accuracy coincides with increased sensitivity to protected attributes, making the accuracy-robustness trade-off explicit.
- Sentiment analysis results show that lexicon-based systems remain stable under both statistical and confounding bias, while biased and random systems amplify biases.
- The group recommendation case study reveals that semantic generalization (taxonomy-based matching) can introduce statistical bias even when simpler matching methods do not.
- In time-series forecasting task, confounding effects are shown to dominate inter-industry comparisons in forecasting.
- Multimodal foundation models that support time-series exhibit lower sensitivity to perturbations after deconfounding, even when they do not achieve the best accuracy.
- The ARC tool translates causal analysis into ratings, allowing users to compare and select models on custom tasks without retraining or access to internal model details.

The Road Ahead

5

Humans are not perfect, and neither is AI. But together, we can create something extraordinary.

— Andrew Ng

5.1 Open Problems

The rapid advancement of AI, particularly the ascendancy of Large Language Models (LLMs) and generative AI architectures, has precipitated a shift in the research landscape. We transitioned from an era defined by the pursuit of capability, measured by performance metrics on static benchmarks, to an era defined by crisis of robust evaluation and verification methods. As models demonstrate increasingly sophisticated behaviors, the AI community faces an inability to rigorously evaluate their trustworthiness, causal reasoning capabilities, and the faithfulness of their explanations (Table 5.1).

5.1.1 Sociotechnical Gaps, Bias, and Robustness Assessment

A primary open problem in AI trust evaluation is the disconnect between technical implementations of trust assessment (e.g., reliability, differential privacy, certified robustness) and the sociotechnical expectations of stakeholders (e.g., justice, epistemic integrity). There is the problem of *validity gap*, where a model may be deemed *robust* by mathematical standards (e.g., satisfying equalized odds) yet remain untrustworthy to affected communities due to historical or contextual factors ignored by the metric [136]. Existing conceptualizations of trust often neglect the *sociotechnical* nature of AI focusing on attributes like reliability and robustness while ignoring dimensions such as *benevolence* (the belief that the system acts in user's best interest) and *integrity* (adherence to a set of ethical principles). Furthermore,

K. Lakkaraju and B. Srivastava, *Assessing, Explaining, and Rating AI Systems for Trust*,
Synthesis Lectures on Computer Science,
https://doi.org/10.1007/978-3-032-21039-5_5

Table 5.1 Key open problems in trustworthy AI, summarizing why they matter in practice and representative emerging research directions

Area	Open problem	Why it matters	Emerging approaches
Bias	Implicit Bias in AI Models	Models may pass explicit safety or alignment evaluation yet still exhibit discriminatory behavior in subtle or indirect ways	Implicit association tests for LLMs; sociotechnical auditing
Causality	Associative v/s Causal Reasoning	LLMs can reproduce causal language patterns without modeling the underlying causal mechanisms	"Fresh" data benchmarks (e.g., CausalProbe-2024); causal abstraction
XAI	Faithfulness v/s Plausibility	Explanations may appear convincing to users while failing to communicate the model's true decision process, leading to misplaced trust	Mechanistic interpretability; faithfulness metrics
General	The Evaluation Gap	The absence of ground truth and reliable automated metrics limits rigorous assessment of model behavior	Human-centered evaluation frameworks; scientifically grounded datasets

a significant proportion of research fails to adequately address the verification (building a product right) and validation (building the right product) of trustworthiness claims. The alignment between actual trustworthiness (system properties) and perceived trustworthiness (user belief) remains poorly understood, leading to challenges in establishing reliable trust in AI systems [136].

There is an immediate need for evaluation methods that can adapt to critical domains like healthcare, where *trust* also implies adherence to medical ethics and explainability protocols. The question that needs to be answered is: *How do we mathematically verify that an AI system respects the institutional norms of the environment it enters?* This remains an unsolved problem.

The transition from discriminative models (e.g., classifiers) to generative models (e.g., LLMs) has rendered the traditional bias assessment methods obsolete.

Models trained to be helpful and harmless often learn to recognize *trap* questions designed to elicit bias and respond with scripted egalitarian statements. However, when prompt is subtle, the underlying bias gets exposed. For example, word association tests have shown that even models that explicitly refuse to state that "women are bad at science" will consistently associate female names with humanities and male names with science in narrative generation tasks. They may recommend candidates with Caucasian names for supervisor positions over equally qualified candidates with Asian names, despite explicitly claiming to be race-blind [20]. This creates a dangerous illusion of fairness. **The open problem here is developing "Implicit Association Tests" (IAT) for AI that can bypass the safety filter to measure the true distribution of associations within the model's parameters**.

Evaluating bias is further complicated by intersectionality and nuances of data representation. Disaggregated evaluation, which measures performance across subgroups, struggles with "curse of dimensionality" when dealing with intersectional identities (e.g., black women with disabilities). The sample size for these specific subgroups in standard evaluation datasets is often too small to yield statistically significant results, leading to their exclusion from analysis and a failure to detect such compounded harms. **Developing evaluation methods to infer bias against small, intersecting subgroups without requiring massive labeled datasets for every combination is a significant open challenge [81]**.

Unlike accuracy, there is no universal ground truth for fairness. Different fairness definitions (e.g., demographic parity vs. individual fairness) are often mathematically incompatible. In the context of LLMs, this problem translates to difficulty of defining what a "fair" generation looks like for an open-ended prompt. The reliance on "LLM-as-a-judge" (using one model to evaluate fairness of another) introduces a recursive bias problem, where the evaluator model's own biases skew the assessment. If GPT-4 is used to evaluate the fairness of Claude 3, GPT-4's implicit biases become the ground truth for fairness. **Breaking this cycle requires independent, sociologically grounded verification methods that do not rely solely on other AI models [172] for evaluation**.

5.1.2 Causal Analysis

A central debate in the AI community is whether LLMs are capable of causal reasoning or are merely *stochastic parrots* mimicking causal language [23]. **Benchmarking this capability is a profound open problem due to the nature of LLM training data**.

Standard benchmarks are often compromised by data contamination. If the causal chain is present in the training data (e.g., historical articles in Wikipedia), the model can answer correctly via pattern matching (associative) rather than causal inference. To reduce training data contamination, recent benchmarks such as CausalProbe-2024 [44] evaluate models on events that occurred after their training cutoff. When tested on this data, models perform substantially worse, particularly on questions that require reasoning about cause and effect. This gap indicates that current LLMs mainly rely on associative patterns, corresponding to the lowest level of Pearl's causal hierarchy, and struggle with intervention-based or counterfactual reasoning. Ongoing work attempts to separate memorization from reasoning using statistical metrics such as Min-K % Probability, which estimates whether a test example closely resembles training data. However, **because LLMs are trained on web-scale corpora with unclear provenance, completely eliminating contamination remains infeasible, making causal evaluation inherently difficult [44].**

5.1.3 Explainable AI (XAI)

The faithfulness v/s plausibility distinction is a central unresolved issue in recent XAI research [6], particularly for generative models. Faithfulness refers to whether an explanation accurately reflects the model's internal decision process, while plausibility refers to whether the explanation is understandable and convincing to a human user. LLMs are increasingly capable of "Chain-of-Thought" (CoT) reasoning, which serves as a form of self-explanation. However, these explanations are optimized for plausibility rather than faithfulness. Research shows that LLMs often generate explanations after deciding on the output, or simply hallucinate a reasoning path that justifies a wrong answer. This is known as *sycophancy* [129, 190] or *unfaithful reasoning*. For example, if a user introduces a bias in the prompt, the LLM might adopt that bias but generate a *neutral-sounding* explanation to cover its tracks. This disconnect means that the *explanation* is effectively a post-hoc rationalization rather than a trace of the decision process [6].

Studies on human-AI collaboration demonstrate a *misinformation effect*, [197] incorrect but convincing explanations significantly impair human decision-making, leading to worse outcomes than if no explanation was provided at all. Worse, this effect degrades the user's own procedural knowledge, after relying on plausible-but-wrong explanations, humans become less capable of performing the task independently. **The open problem is designing explanations that aid decision-making without inducing over-reliance or degrading human expertise [197].**

Measuring faithfulness in generative models is far harder than in classification models (where feature importance can be tested via ablation). One proposed method is to check for self-consistency [126]. If the model says feature X is important, does removing feature X change the output? However, such simple perturbations can be unreliable as LLMs are more robust to them. New metrics like *Counterfactual Simulatability* [43] and *Causal Faithfulness* [171] are being developed, but they are computationally expensive and arguably still proxy measures.

In XAI, we rarely have *ground truth explanations*. When an AI system produces an incorrect outcome, it is often unclear whether the error comes from the model's prediction or from the explanation method itself. Because explanation methods add another layer of complexity on top of an already black-box model, failures in prediction and failures in explanation are difficult to separate.

Since explanations are for humans, human evaluation is the gold standard. However, it is fraught with difficulties. Recent systematic reviews propose frameworks like the 6-pillar framework [7] to standardize user studies, focusing on constructs like mental models, user satisfaction, and task performance. However, few studies currently adhere to these standards, leading to a literature filled with incomparable results.

Most user studies are conducted in lab settings with low stakes. There is a lack of "in-the-wild" evaluation in critical domains like finance and healthcare where the cost of misplaced trust is high. Application-grounded evaluation is expensive and legally complex to organize [7, 91].

To bypass unreliability in post-hoc explanations, a sub-field called *Mechanistic Interpretability* aims to reverse-engineer the neural network into human-understandable algorithms (circuits). A major problem in this domain is *polysemanticity*. Single neurons often activate multiple, unrelated concepts (e.g., a neuron responding to both "cats" and "cars"). This occurs due to *superposition*, where the model compresses more features than it has dimensions [103]. A leading approach to solving this is training sparse autoencoders (SAEs) to disentangle these superpositioned features into a sparse, interpretable basis. However, determining the correct *dictionary size* for SAEs is an open problem. If the dictionary is too small, features remain entangled, if too large, they split into uninterpretable fragments [97]. While successful on small models, scaling mechanistic interpretability to frontier models (e.g., GPT-4) remains a daunting challenge. We currently lack the tools to automatically identify and verify millions of circuits without human intervention [9].

5.2 What We Have Learned

In this section, we reflect on observations that emerged while applying ARC across different tasks.

1. **Accuracy Alone is Insufficient for Trust**
   High accuracy in an AI model does not guarantee that the model is stable or fair. One critical aspect of trustworthiness is robustness, defined as an AI model's limited sensitivity to protected attributes (bias) and to input perturbations (instability). Without this multi-dimensional evaluation, models that appear accurate may actually exhibit sensitivity to noise or protected attributes that remains invisible under standard accuracy metrics.
2. **Limitations of Current Explainable AI (XAI) Need to be Overcome**
   Most current XAI techniques provide static, *one-shot* explanations that justify a model's output rather than supporting a user's natural reasoning process. A distinction must be made between *interpretability*, which is an inherent property of white-box models (like decision trees), and *explainability*, which relies on external post-hoc methods to approximate the behavior of black-box models. Furthermore, explanations are often

treated as a destination rather than a process, failing to answer broader questions about a model's overall fairness or stability.

3. **There is Necessity of Causal Reasoning in Assessment**
   Causality is required to move beyond simple correlations and spurious associations, which often lead to misleading or unfair decisions in critical domains like finance. Following Pearl's "Ladder of Causation," reasoning must progress from *Association* (observing correlations) to *Intervention* (acting on variables) and finally to *Counterfactuals* (imagining alternate realities) to truly understand model behavior. This causal framing helps distinguish between variables that co-occur and those that actually produce an effect.
4. **Structural Causal Models and Confounding are Needed**
   A Structural Causal Model (SCM) allows for the specification of how variables, such as protected attributes (Z), treatments (T), and outcomes (O), influence one another. This setup is critical for identifying *confounders*, which are variables that influence both the treatment and the outcome, creating *backdoor paths* that induce spurious associations. To estimate true causal effects, these backdoor paths must be blocked using adjustment methods like conditioning or propensity score matching.
5. **Limitations of Causal Models Need to be Overcome**
   Causal identification refers to the ability to express a causal quantity of interest, such as the effect of a treatment on an outcome, using only the observed data and a specified causal model. Identification determines whether a causal effect can be computed in principle, assuming infinite data, given the assumed relationships among variables. When a causal effect is not identified, no statistical method can recover it from the available observations without additional assumptions or information. A key limitation of causal modeling is that identification depends on assumptions about which variables are observed and how they are related. In many settings, various relevant factors are unobserved, measured indirectly, or excluded due to data constraints. If such attributes influence both the treatment and the outcome, the causal effect is not identified under standard adjustment methods, even though estimates may still be produced numerically. As a result, the conclusions must be interpreted as conditional on the stated model assumptions rather than as unconditional statements about the system.
6. **We introduce the ARC Framework (AI Rating through Causality)**
   The ARC framework treats robustness as a multi-dimensional property of an AI model, encompassing sensitivity to protected attributes, sensitivity to perturbations, and the influence of confounding variables. It employs a fixed causal setup to quantify these elements and compares models against baselines, such as random and biased models, to provide context for the results. The goal of ARC is to help users select the right model for a specific task and dataset by expressing robustness measures as ratings.

7. **Three Key Robustness Metrics are Used**
   The rating method relies on three primary metrics to quantify model robustness:

   - **Weighted Rejection Score (WRS):** Quantifies statistical bias by testing if outcomes differ significantly across protected groups (e.g., gender or age).
   - **Deconfounding Impact Estimate (DIE%) or Propensity Score Matching—DIE (PIE %):** Measures confounding bias by calculating how much the estimated treatment effect changes after adjusting for confounders.
   - **Average Treatment Effect (ATE):** Estimates the causal impact of interventions (treatments) on the model's outcome after removing confounding influences.

8. **A Rating Workflow is Introduced**
   The rating process consists of two stages: *Data-to-Predictions*, where models generate outputs under perturbed and unperturbed conditions, and *Predictions-to-Ratings*, where statistical and causal analyses convert raw scores into ratings. Raw scores are used to construct a partial order of models for each metric, which are then discretized into final rating levels to allow for easy comparison across different AI systems.
9. **There is a Trade-off Between Accuracy and Robustness**
   Applying ARC to tasks like credit risk assessment exposes an explicit trade-off: complex models like Random Forests may achieve higher accuracy but often exhibit greater bias (sensitivity to protected attributes) compared to simpler models like Logistic Regression. While Logistic Regression may perform slightly worse on accuracy metrics, it can demonstrate greater stability and lower confounding bias. ARC uses Pareto frontiers to visualize these trade-offs, helping users identify models that optimally balance performance and robustness.
10. **Bias is Context-Dependent**
    Lessons learned from applying ARC across diverse tasks, including sentiment analysis and group recommendation, show that no model class is uniformly better or worse; bias is task- and method-dependent. For example, in group recommendation, a taxonomy-based semantic matching method introduced statistical bias by amplifying existing data structures, whereas simpler string matching did not. Similarly, in time-series forecasting, *Industry* was found to be a stronger source of confounding bias than *Company*.
11. **Ratings serve as Decision Support**
    In ARC, ratings are used to compare models under the same causal assumptions. They show how models differ with respect to bias, confounding, and sensitivity to perturbations. The ratings do not decide which model should be used. They simply make these differences visible so that users can consider them alongside task requirements and practical constraints.

5.3 Emerging Regulatory Paradigms and Safe Deployment Strategies for AI in Financial Services

While finance industry has long leveraged predictive analytics and ML for tasks such as trading and fraud detection, the advent of Generative AI (GenAI) and LLMs has catalyzed a transformation in architectures, customer engagement models, and risk management paradigms. This technological transformation led to the emergence of *agentic* capabilities, systems that do not simply analyze data but actively formulate strategies, execute transactions, and generate sophisticated financial content. The deployment of such stochastic, non-deterministic models in critical financial environments introduce risks that traditional governance frameworks are ill-equipped to manage. Issues ranging from hallucination in financial reporting to the amplification of bias in credit scoring have moved from theoretical concerns to operational challenges that need to be addressed immediately [237]. The years 2023 to 2025 have witnessed the crystallization of global regulatory standards, most notable European Union's AI Act (EU AI Act), and the proliferation of sophisticated compliance strategies designed to align AI performance with ethical mandates.

The regulatory environment for AI in finance is currently defined by a geopolitical bifurcation. On one side stands the EU with a centralized legislative model, on the other side is the USA with decentralized, sector-specific approach driven by agency guidance. Understanding the nuances, intersections, and contradictions of these regimes is a prerequisite for any financial institution operating in the global market.

5.3.1 The European Union (EU): Centralized AI Act

The enforcement of EU AI Act represents a watershed moment in the history of AI regulation. It establishes the world's first legal framework for AI, classifying systems based on the severity of risk they pose to fundamental rights and safety [3].

The AI Act's risk-based architecture is its defining feature. Unless used solely for the purpose of detection of financial fraud, AI systems deployed in finance are designated as "high-risk." Providers of such high-risk AI systems are mandated to implement a continuous risk management system that operates throughout the entire lifecycle of the AI, from design and development to deployment. Furthermore, the Act imposes strict data governance requirements. Firms must ensure that training, validation, and testing datasets are relevant, representative, and free of errors to the best extent possible [16]. Transparency and record-keeping requirements under the Act are equally stringent. Documentation must be sufficiently detailed to allow regulatory authorities to interpret the system's output and verify its compliance with the law [60]. This effectively mandates a level of explainability that may preclude the use of certain black-box deep learning architectures in credit scoring unless their decision-making logic can be made intelligible to human auditors [164].

The Act also delineates "unacceptable risk" categories that are prohibited outright. In the financial context, this ban extends to AI systems that deploy subliminal techniques to distort behavior or exploit vulnerabilities related to age or socioeconomic status.

EU AI Act regulation not only to firms based in the EU, but also to any provider that places an AI system on the EU market, deploys it within the EU, or uses its outputs to support decisions affecting the EU. As a result, financial institutions headquartered outside Europe may still fall under the Act if their AI systems interact with EU markets or customers. This broad scope is expected to produce a "Brussels Effect," as multinational firms are likely to adopt EU requirements across their global operations to avoid the cost and complexity of maintaining region-specific compliance frameworks. Consequently, researchers argue that the EU AI Act is likely to function as a de facto global standard for AI governance in finance, shaping development and governance practices in major financial centers such as New York, London, and Singapore [104].

5.3.2 The USA: A Sector-Specific Approach

The USA regulatory strategy relies on external federal agencies interpreting their statutory authorities to cover new AI technologies, reinforced by executive actions that prioritize innovation and market stability alongside consumer protection. President Biden's Executive Order 14110 on the "Safe, Secure, and Trustworthy Development and Use of Artificial Intelligence" (issued in late 2023) marked a pivotal attempt to coordinate this decentralized strategy. The order directs a "whole-of-government" response, mandating the agencies such as the Consumer Financial Protection Bureau (CFBP), the Federal Housing Finance Agency (FHFA), and the Federal Trade Commission (FTC) vigorously enforce existing consumer protection and civil rights laws in the context of AI [104]. The Order requires agencies to issue guidance on how landmark statutes like the Equal Credit Opportunity Act (ECOA) and the Fair Housing Act apply to AI-driven decisions, effectively signaling that the black-box nature of AI is no defense against liability for discriminatory outcomes [119].

The CFBP has emerged as a particularly active regulator in this domain, asserting that "technology is not an excuse for law-breaking." In a series of circulars and guidance documents issues throughout 2023 and 2024, the Bureau clarified that lenders must provide specific and accurate reasons for credit denials, even when those decisions are based on complex algorithmic models [135]. The "Consumer Financial Protection Circular 2024–06" is a crucial document in this regard. It addressed the use of background dossiers and algorithmic scores for employment and hiring, reinforcing that the Fair Credit Reporting Act (FCRA) applies to these automated assessments. The circular warns that employers and third-party providers must comply with FCRA obligations, including obtaining worker permission and providing adverse action notices [46]. The CFBP's position effectively mandates *explainability* for adverse actions, a lender cannot simply state that "the model denied the loan" but must articulate the specific variables (e.g., debt-to-income ratio, payment history) that drove the decision.

The U.S. Department of Treasury has complemented this approach with a focus on systemic risk. In its 2024 reports, the treasury identified key vulnerabilities associated with AI adoption, including the risks of third-party dependency and the potential for "herding behavior" where correlated algorithmic trading strategies amplify market volatility [62].

5.3.3 Comparing AI Regulatory Frameworks in the U.S. and EU

EU model is characterized as "rights-driven," prioritizing precautionary principle and the protection of fundamental rights through ex-ante regulation. It seeks to prevent harm before it occurs by imposing strict requirements on the development and deployment of high-risk systems [52]. Conversely, the US model is described as "market-driven," prioritizing innovation, efficiency and the handling market failures through ex-post enforcement. It assumes that existing laws sufficiently handle new technologies and that overly prescriptive regulation could stifle American competitiveness in the global AI race [52]. A model that is compliant with US fair lending laws might not satisfy the EU AI Act's technical documentation and data governance standards. This will lead to a fragmented compliance environment where firms may be forced to bifurcate their AI operations or, more likely, adopt the strictest common denominator (the EU standard).

5.3.4 The Rise of Agentic Workflows

With the rise of agentic workflows, AI systems increasingly act as autonomous components within the financial ecosystem. These "FinAgents" [232] can autonomously execute multi-step workflows: searching for data, analyzing it, formulating a strategy, and executing trades or generating regulatory reports without human intervention. Such autonomy introduces new complexities for regulation. When an AI agent executes a chain of decisions: search, analyze, trade, the "decision" is no longer a single output but a sequence of actions. Tracing accountability in such workflows is difficult, especially if the agent interacts with other agents in market environment, potentially leading to emergent behaviors like algorithmic collusion or flash crashes (arising from fast-paced decision making and ineffective guardrails) that were not programmed by the developers [89].

The shift in the role of AI from decision support to automated action taker will make the task of evaluating AI harder, and of ensuring safety virtually impossible, since the *world* would change after the action is executed. In such a situation, any guarantee will require constraints to be put on actions or the environment. We envisage that more methods from the well studied field of automated planning and robotics [68] will become relevant for AI assessment here in future.

5.3.5 Algorithm Risks in Finance

Hallucination, the generation of plausible but factually incorrect information, is identified as the single most critical barrier to the safe deployment of GenAI in finance. In financial reporting or investment analysis, a numerical error is a regulatory violation or a source of significant financial loss [237]. The Financial Stability Board (FSB) and IMF have warned of herding behavior, where multiple AI models, trained on similar datasets and optimizing for similar objective functions, converge on identical trading strategies. This correlation can make market volatility during stress periods even worse, leading to liquidity crunches and asset price spirals [62].

5.3.6 Frameworks for Safe Deployment of AI

To mitigate AI risks and align with the emerging regulatory landscape, researchers have developed robust frameworks that move beyond simple compliance checklists. The "Artificial Intelligence Governance Framework for Finance" (AIGF-F) represents a "control-by-design" philosophy. This framework argues that governance cannot be reactive supervisory function but must be embedded into the system architecture itself [156]. Recognizing the fluid nature of AI regulation, the framework includes dynamic monitoring tools that update compliance parameters as regulations change. If a new fairness metric becomes a regulatory standard, the system's internal audit function is updated to optimize for that metric without requiring complete build of the model.

Traditional Model Risk Management (MRM) frameworks, such as the US Federal Reserve's SR 11-7, are being adapted for the stochastic nature of GenAI. [29] introduces an "end-to-end GenAI model risk management framework" that introducing incremental testing pillars. This involves deep scrutiny of foundation models from their selection to evaluating the process of decision-making using techniques like CoT prompting, that forces the model to display its reasoning path. It also assessing the robustness of these models and detecting hallucinations using automated metrics to score faithfulness of the output against the source documents.

5.4 Chapter Summary

This chapter discusses the technical and regulatory insights developed throughout the book, identifying where current AI evaluation methods succeed, where they fail, and what these limits imply for real-world financial deployment.

- High accuracy does not guarantee robustness, as models can remain sensitive to protected attributes, confounders, or small input perturbations that standard benchmarks fail to reveal.
- Generative models frequently pass explicit fairness checks while still exhibiting implicit bias in indirect tasks, creating a false sense of alignment and safety.
- Intersectional bias remains difficult to evaluate in practice because subgroup-level (e.g., African women with disabilities) analysis breaks down under data sparsity, leading to systematic exclusion of the most vulnerable groups from assessment.
- LLMs often produce correct causal statements without performing causal reasoning, relying instead on learned associations that collapse under intervention-based or post-training evaluation.
- Causal evaluation is inherently constrained by data contamination and non-identification, meaning many effects of interest cannot be recovered without strong, explicit assumptions.
- Explanations generated by modern AI systems tend to optimize for human plausibility rather than faithfulness to the underlying decision process, which can mislead users and degrade decision quality.
- Faithful explanation of generative models remains unresolved, as existing metrics are indirect, computationally expensive, and lack ground-truth reference points.
- Emerging regulatory frameworks in the EU and U.S. increasingly require explainability, traceability, and risk management guarantees that exceed the capabilities of many current evaluation methods.

References

The references span a wide variety of academic material in AI (reasoning, learning, LLMs), collaborative assistants (chatbots), software engineering, AI trustworthiness, and causal reasoning.

References

1. Abdin, M., Jacobs, S.A., Awan, A.A., Aneja, J., Awadallah, A., Awadalla, H., Bach, N., Bahree, A., Bakhtiari, A., Behl, H.: Phi-3 technical report: a highly capable language model locally on your phone (2024). arXiv preprint arXiv:2404.14219
2. Achiam, J., Adler, S., Agarwal, S., Ahmad, L., Akkaya, I., Aleman, F.L., Almeida, D., Altenschmidt, J., Altman, S., Anadkat, S.: Gpt-4 technical report (2023). arXiv preprint arXiv:2303.08774
3. Act, E.A.I.: The EU Artificial Intelligence Act. European Union (2024)
4. Addy, W.A., Ajayi-Nifise, A.O., Bello, B.G., Tula, S.T., Odeyemi, O., Falaiye, T.: Ai in credit scoring: a comprehensive review of models and predictive analytics. Glob. J. Eng. Technol. Adv. **18**(02), 118–129 (2024)
5. Agar, J.: What is science for? the lighthill report on artificial intelligence reinterpreted. Br. J. Hist. Sci. **53**(3), 289–310 (2020)
6. Agarwal, C., Tanneru, S.H., Lakkaraju, H.: Faithfulness vs. plausibility: on the (un) reliability of explanations from large language models (2024). arXiv preprint arXiv:2402.04614
7. Al-Ansari, N., Al-Thani, D., Al-Mansoori, R.S.: User-centered evaluation of explainable artificial intelligence (xai): a systematic literature review. Hum. Behav. Emerg. Technol. **2024**(1), 4628855 (2024)
8. Aldasoro, I., Gambacorta, L., Korinek, A., Shreeti, V., Stein, M.: Intelligent financial system: how AI is transforming finance. Bank for International Settlements, Monetary and Economic Department (2024)

K. Lakkaraju and B. Srivastava, *Assessing, Explaining, and Rating AI Systems for Trust*, Synthesis Lectures on Computer Science, https://doi.org/10.1007/978-3-032-21039-5

9. Andersen, M.F., Heuss, M., Lucic, A.: Three desiderata for faithfulness in machine learning explanations: the case for causal abstraction. In: Mechanistic Interpretability Workshop at NeurIPS (2025)
10. Angrist, J.D., Imbens, G.W., Rubin, D.B.: Identification of causal effects using instrumental variables. J. Am. Stat. Assoc. **91**(434), 444–455 (1996)
11. Anil, R., Dai, A.M., Firat, O., Johnson, M., Lepikhin, D., Passos, A., Shakeri, S., Taropa, E., Bailey, P., Chen, Z.: Palm 2 technical report (2023). arXiv preprint arXiv:2305.10403
12. Ansari, A.F., Stella, L., Turkmen, C., Zhang, X., Mercado, P., Shen, H., Shchur, O., Rangapuram, S.S., Arango, S.P., Kapoor, S.: Chronos: learning the language of time series (2024). arXiv preprint arXiv:2403.07815
13. Apley, D.W., Zhu, J.: Visualizing the effects of predictor variables in black box supervised learning models. J. R. Stat. Soc. Ser. B Stat Methodol. **82**(4), 1059–1086 (2020)
14. Arrieta, A.B., Díaz-Rodríguez, N., Del Ser, J., Bennetot, A., Tabik, S., Barbado, A., García, S., Gil-López, S., Molina, D., Benjamins, R., et al.: Explainable artificial intelligence (XAI): concepts, taxonomies, opportunities and challenges toward responsible AI. Inf. Fusion **58**, 82–115 (2020)
15. Arsenault, P.D., Wang, S., Patenaude, J.M.: A survey of explainable artificial intelligence (XAI) in financial time series forecasting. ACM Comput. Surv. **57**(10), 1–37 (2025)
16. Artificial Intelligence Act: High-level summary of the EU artificial intelligence act. https://artificialintelligenceact.eu/high-level-summary/ (2024), accessed: December 2025
17. Asimov, I.: Runaround. I, Robot. Bantam Dell (1950)
18. Atrey, P., Brundage, M.P., Wu, M., Dutta, S.: Demystifying the accuracy-interpretability trade-off: a case study of inferring ratings from reviews (2025). arXiv preprint arXiv:2503.07914
19. Bach, S., Binder, A., Montavon, G., Klauschen, F., Müller, K.R., Samek, W.: On pixel-wise explanations for non-linear classifier decisions by layer-wise relevance propagation. PLoS ONE **10**(7), e0130140 (2015)
20. Bai, X., Wang, A., Sucholutsky, I., Griffiths, T.L.: Explicitly unbiased large language models still form biased associations. Proc. Natl. Acad. Sci. **122**(8), e2416228122 (2025)
21. Bang, H., Robins, J.M.: Doubly robust estimation in missing data and causal inference models. Biometrics **61**(4), 962–973 (2005)
22. Bellamy, R.K.E., Dey, K., Hind, M., Hoffman, S.C., Houde, S., Kannan, K., Lohia, P., Martino, J., Mehta, S., Mojsilovic, A., Nagar, S., Ramamurthy, K.N., Richards, J., Saha, D., Sattigeri, P., Singh, M., Varshney, K.R., Zhang, Y.: Ai fairness 360: an extensible toolkit for detecting, understanding, and mitigating unwanted algorithmic bias (2018)
23. Bender, E.M., Gebru, T., McMillan-Major, A., Shmitchell, S.: On the dangers of stochastic parrots: can language models be too big? In: Proceedings of the 2021 ACM Conference on Fairness, Accountability, and Transparency, pp. 610–623 (2021)
24. Bernagozzi, M., Srivastava, B., Rossi, F., Usmani, S.: Gender bias in online language translators: visualization, human perception, and bias/accuracy trade-offs. In: In IEEE Internet Computing, Special Issue on Sociotechnical Perspectives, Nov/Dec (2021)
25. Bernagozzi, M., Srivastava, B., Rossi, F., Usmani, S.: Gender bias in online language translators: visualization, human perception, and bias/accuracy tradeoffs. IEEE Internet Comput. **25**(5), 53–63 (2021). https://doi.org/10.1109/MIC.2021.3097604
26. Bernagozzi, M., Srivastava, B., Rossi, F., Usmani, S.: Vega: a virtual environment for exploring gender bias vs. accuracy trade-offs in ai translation services. In: Proceedings of the AAAI Conference on Artificial Intelligence, vol. 35(18), pp. 15994–15996 (May 2021), https://ojs.aaai.org/index.php/AAAI/article/view/17991
27. Bernagozzi, M., Srivastava, B., Rossi, F., Usmani, S.: Vega: a virtual environment for exploring gender bias vs. accuracy trade-offs in AI translation services. In: Proceedings of the AAAI

Conference on Artificial Intelligence, vol. 35(18), pp. 15994–15996 (May 2021).https://doi.org/10.1609/aaai.v35i18.17991, https://ojs.aaai.org/index.php/AAAI/article/view/17991

28. Bhatt, U., Xiang, A., Sharma, S., Weller, A., Taly, A., Jia, Y., Ghosh, J., Puri, R., Moura, J.M., Eckersley, P.: Explainable machine learning in deployment. In: Proceedings of the 2020 Conference on Fairness, Accountability, and Transparency, pp. 648–657 (2020)
29. Bhattacharyya, A., Yu, Y., Yang, H., Singh, R., Joshi, T., Chen, J., Yalavarthy, K.: Model risk management for generative AI in financial institutions (2025). arXiv preprint arXiv:2503.15668
30. Bird, S., Dudík, M., Edgar, R., Horn, B., Lutz, R., Milan, V., Sameki, M., Wallach, H., Walker, K.: Fairlearn: a toolkit for assessing and improving fairness in AI. Microsoft, Tech. Rep. MSR-TR-2020-32 (2020)
31. Blöbaum, P., Götz, P., Budhathoki, K., Mastakouri, A.A., Janzing, D.: Dowhy-gcm: an extension of dowhy for causal inference in graphical causal models. J. Mach. Learn. Res. **25**(147), 1–7 (2024)
32. Board of Governors of the Federal Reserve System: Sr 11-7: Guidance on model risk management. https://www.federalreserve.gov/supervisionreg/srletters/sr1107.htm (2011), accessed: 2025-08-27
33. Bondielli, A., Passaro, L.C.: Leveraging clip for image emotion recognition. In: CEUR Workshop Proceedings, vol. 3015. CEUR-WS (2021)
34. Brown, T., Mann, B., Ryder, N., Subbiah, M., Kaplan, J.D., Dhariwal, P., Neelakantan, A., Shyam, P., Sastry, G., Askell, A., et al.: Language models are few-shot learners. Adv. Neural. Inf. Process. Syst. **33**, 1877–1901 (2020)
35. Buolamwini, J., Gebru, T.: Gender shades: Intersectional accuracy disparities in commercial gender classification. In: Friedler, S.A., Wilson, C. (eds.): Conference on Fairness, Accountability and Transparency, FAT 2018, 23-24 February 2018, New York, NY, USA. Proceedings of Machine Learning Research, vol. 81, pp. 77–91. PMLR (2018). http://proceedings.mlr.press/v81/buolamwini18a.html
36. Carloni, G., Berti, A., Colantonio, S.: The role of causality in explainable artificial intelligence. Wiley Interdiscip. Rev.: Data Min. Knowl. Discov. **15**(2), e70015 (2025)
37. Catal, M., Günther, M.: Advsecurenet: a python toolkit for adversarial machine learning (2024). arXiv preprint arXiv:2409.02629
38. Cavique, L.: Implications of causality in artificial intelligence. Front. Artif. Intell. **7**, 1439702 (2024)
39. Černevičienė, J., Kabašinskas, A.: Explainable artificial intelligence (XAI) in finance: a systematic literature review. Artif. Intell. Rev. **57**(8), 216 (2024)
40. Chai, J., Lu, S., Wang, X.: Identifying and mitigating spurious correlation in multi-task learning. In: Proceedings of the Computer Vision and Pattern Recognition Conference, pp. 25698–25707 (2025)
41. Chen, H., Harinen, T., Lee, J.Y., Yung, M., Zhao, Z.: Causalml: Python package for causal machine learning (2020). arXiv preprint arXiv:2002.11631
42. Chen, X.Q., Ma, C.Q., Ren, Y.S., Lei, Y.T., Huynh, N.Q.A., Narayan, S.: Explainable artificial intelligence in finance: a bibliometric review. Financ. Res. Lett. **56**, 104145 (2023)
43. Chen, Y., Zhong, R., Ri, N., Zhao, C., He, H., Steinhardt, J., Yu, Z., McKeown, K.: Do models explain themselves? counterfactual simulatability of natural language explanations. arXiv preprint arXiv:2307.08678 (2023)
44. Chi, H., Li, H., Yang, W., Liu, F., Lan, L., Ren, X., Liu, T., Han, B.: Unveiling causal reasoning in large language models: reality or mirage? Adv. Neural. Inf. Process. Syst. **37**, 96640–96670 (2024)
45. Comeau, M., Thulasiraman, K.: Algorithms on marked directed graphs. Can. Electr. Eng. J. **9**(2), 72–80 (1984)

46. Consumer Financial Protection Bureau: Consumer financial protection circular 2024–06: Background dossiers and algorithmic scores for hiring, promotion, and other employment decisions. https://www.consumerfinance.gov/compliance/circulars/consumer-financial-protection-circular-2024-06-background-dossiers-and-algorithmic-scores-for-hiring-promotion-and-other-employment-decisions/ (2024), consumer Financial Protection Circular
47. Cordeschi, R.: AI turns fifty: revisiting its origins. Appl. Artif. Intell. **21**(4–5), 259–279 (2007)
48. Craven, M., Shavlik, J.: Extracting tree-structured representations of trained networks. Adv. Neural. Inf. Process. Syst. **8** (1995)
49. Datta, A., Fredrikson, M., Ko, G., Mardziel, P., Sen, S.: Proxy non-discrimination in data-driven systems (2017). arXiv preprint arXiv:1707.08120
50. Daubechies, I.: The wavelet transform, time-frequency localization and signal analysis. IEEE Trans. Inf. Theory **36**(5), 961–1005 (1990)
51. Davidson, T., Warmsley, D., Macy, M., Weber, I.: Automated hate speech detection and the problem of offensive language. In: Proceedings of the International AAAI Conference on Web and Social Media, vol. 11, pp. 512–515 (2017)
52. Davtyan, T.: The us approach to AI regulation: federal laws, policies, and strategies explained. J. Law Technol. Internet **16**(2), 223 (2025)
53. De Kleer, J.: An assumption-based TMS. Artif. Intell. **28**(2), 127–162 (1986)
54. Demajo, L.M., Vella, V., Dingli, A.: Explainable AI for interpretable credit scoring (2020). arXiv preprint arXiv:2012.03749
55. Dhawan, R., Shay, D.: Principles of causation. StatPearls (2024)
56. Doyle, J.: A truth maintenance system. Artif. Intell. **12**(3), 231–272 (1979)
57. Driscoll, P.J., Parnell, G.S., Henderson, D.L.: Decision Making in Systems Engineering and Management. Wiley (2022)
58. Dua, D., Graff, C.: UCI machine learning repository (2017). http://archive.ics.uci.edu/ml
59. Dung, P.T., Giudici, P.: Sustainability, accuracy, fairness, and explainability (safe) machine learning in quantitative trading. Mathematics **13**(3), 442 (2025)
60. Eurofi: AI act: Key measures and implications for financial services. https://www.eurofi.net/wp-content/uploads/2024/12/ii.2-ai-act-key-measures-and-implications-for-financial-services.pdf (December 2024), accessed: December 2025
61. Fawkes, J., Fishman, N., Andrews, M., Lipton, Z.: The fragility of fairness: causal sensitivity analysis for fair machine learning. Adv. Neural. Inf. Process. Syst. **37**, 137105–137134 (2024)
62. Financial Stability Board: The financial stability implications of artificial intelligence. https://www.fsb.org/2024/11/the-financial-stability-implications-of-artificial-intelligence/ (November 2024), fSB report
63. Fok, J.L., Zeng, Q., Chen, S., Fawkes, O., Chen, H.: Foe for fraud: Transferable adversarial attacks in credit card fraud detection. arXiv preprint arXiv:2508.14699 (2025)
64. Frank, A.: UCI machine learning repository. http://archive.ics.uci.edu/ml (2010)
65. Friedman, J.H.: Greedy function approximation: a gradient boosting machine. Ann. Stat. 1189–1232 (2001)
66. Furlanello, T., Lipton, Z., Tschannen, M., Itti, L., Anandkumar, A.: Born again neural networks. In: International Conference on Machine Learning, pp. 1607–1616. PMLR (2018)
67. Fuster, A., Goldsmith-Pinkham, P., Ramadorai, T., Walther, A.: Predictably unequal? the effects of machine learning on credit markets. J. Financ. **77**(1), 5–47 (2022)
68. Ghallab, M., Nau, D., Traverso, P.: Automated Planning: Theory and Practice. The Morgan Kaufmann Series in Artificial Intelligence. Morgan Kaufmann, Amsterdam (2004). http://www.sciencedirect.com/science/book/9781558608566
69. Giudici, P., Centurelli, M., Turchetta, S.: Artificial intelligence risk measurement. Expert Syst. Appl. **235**, 121220 (2024)

70. Goethals, S., Martens, D., Calders, T.: Precof: counterfactual explanations for fairness. Mach. Learn. **113**(5), 3111–3142 (2024)
71. Goldstein, A., Kapelner, A., Bleich, J., Pitkin, E.: Peeking inside the black box: visualizing statistical learning with plots of individual conditional expectation. J. Comput. Graph. Stat. **24**(1), 44–65 (2015)
72. Goodfellow, I.J., Pouget-Abadie, J., Mirza, M., Xu, B., Warde-Farley, D., Ozair, S., Courville, A., Bengio, Y.: Generative adversarial nets. In: Advances in Neural Information Processing Systems, p. 27 (2014)
73. Goswami, M., Szafer, K., Choudhry, A., Cai, Y., Li, S., Dubrawski, A.: Moment: a family of open time-series foundation models (2024). arXiv preprint arXiv:2402.03885
74. Gramegna, A., Giudici, P.: Shap and lime: an evaluation of discriminative power in credit risk. Front. Artif. Intell. **4**, 752558 (2021)
75. Gunning, D., Aha, D.: Darpa's explainable artificial intelligence (XAI) program. AI Mag. **40**(2), 44–58 (2019)
76. Gurumoorthy, K.S., Dhurandhar, A., Cecchi, G., Aggarwal, C.: Efficient data representation by selecting prototypes with importance weights. In: 2019 IEEE International Conference on Data Mining (ICDM), pp. 260–269. IEEE (2019)
77. Hatt, T., Feuerriegel, S.: Sequential deconfounding for causal inference with unobserved confounders. In: Causal Learning and Reasoning, pp. 934–956. PMLR (2024)
78. He, K., Zhang, X., Ren, S., Sun, J.: Deep residual learning for image recognition. In: Proceedings of the IEEE Conference on Computer Vision and Pattern Recognition, pp. 770–778 (2016)
79. Heinze-Deml, C., Maathuis, M.H., Meinshausen, N.: Causal structure learning. Annu. Rev. Stat. Appl. **5**(1), 371–391 (2018)
80. Henderson, P., Sinha, K., Angelard-Gontier, N., Ke, N.R., Fried, G., Lowe, R., Pineau, J.: Ethical challenges in data-driven dialogue systems. In: Proceedings of the 2018 AAAI/ACM Conference on AI, Ethics, and Society, pp. 123–129 (2018)
81. Herlihy, C., Truong, K., Chouldechova, A., Dudík, M.: A structured regression approach for evaluating model performance across intersectional subgroups. In: Proceedings of the 2024 ACM Conference on Fairness, Accountability, and Transparency, pp. 313–325. (2024)
82. Hill, A.B.: The environment and disease: association or causation? (1965)
83. Hinton, G.E., Salakhutdinov, R.R.: Reducing the dimensionality of data with neural networks. Science **313**(5786), 504–507 (2006)
84. Hochreiter, S., Schmidhuber, J.: Long short-term memory. Neural Comput. **9**(8), 1735–1780 (1997)
85. Hoffman, R.R., Miller, T., Klein, G., Mueller, S.T., Clancey, W.J.: Increasing the value of XAI for users: a psychological perspective. KI-Künstliche Intelligenz **37**(2), 237–247 (2023)
86. Hurley, M., Adebayo, J.: Credit scoring in the era of big data. Yale JL & Tech. **18**, 148 (2016)
87. Hurst, A., Lerer, A., Goucher, A.P., Perelman, A., Ramesh, A., Clark, A., Ostrow, A., Welihinda, A., Hayes, A., Radford, A.: Gpt-4o system card (2024). arXiv preprint arXiv:2410.21276
88. Hutto, C.J., Folds, D.J., Appling, S.: Computationally detecting and quantifying the degree of bias in sentence-level text of news stories. In: The First International Conference on Human and Social Analytics (HUSO) (2015)
89. International Monetary Fund, Monetary and Capital Markets Department: Advances in artificial intelligence: Implications for capital market activities. In: Global Financial Stability Report, chap. 3. International Monetary Fund, Washington, DC (October 2024). https://doi.org/10.5089/9798400277573.082.CH003, accessed: December 23, 2025
90. Jain, S., Wallace, B.C.: Attention is not explanation (2019). arXiv preprint arXiv:1902.10186
91. Jesus, S., Belém, C., Balayan, V., Bento, J., Saleiro, P., Bizarro, P., Gama, J.: How can i choose an explainer? an application-grounded evaluation of post-hoc explanations. In: Proceedings of the 2021 ACM conference on fairness, accountability, and transparency, pp. 805–815 (2021)

92. Jiang, J., Leofante, F., Rago, A., Toni, F.: Formalising the robustness of counterfactual explanations for neural networks. In: Proceedings of the AAAI Conference on Artificial Intelligence, vol. 37, pp. 14901–14909 (2023)
93. Jiang, J., Leofante, F., Rago, A., Toni, F.: Robust counterfactual explanations in machine learning: a survey (2024). arXiv preprint arXiv:2402.01928
94. Johnson, B., Brun, Y.: Fairkit-learn: a fairness evaluation and comparison toolkit. In: Proceedings of the ACM/IEEE 44th International Conference on Software Engineering: Companion Proceedings, pp. 70–74 (2022)
95. Jones, C.R., Bergen, B.K.: Large language models pass the turing test (2025). arXiv preprint arXiv:2503.23674
96. Karlgren, J., Höök, K., Lantz, A., Palme, J., Pargman, D.: The glass box user model for filtering, Swedish Institute of Computer Science (1994)
97. Karvonen, A., Rager, C., Lin, J., Tigges, C., Bloom, J., Chanin, D., Lau, Y.T., Farrell, E., McDougall, C., Ayonrinde, K., et al.: Saebench: a comprehensive benchmark for sparse autoencoders in language model interpretability. arXiv preprint arXiv:2503.09532 (2025)
98. Keshri, M.K.: Bloomberggpt: Revolutionizing finance with large language models. Available at SSRN, 5215949 (2025)
99. Kiritchenko, S., Mohammad, S.: Examining gender and race bias in two hundred sentiment analysis systems. In: Proceedings of the Seventh Joint Conference on Lexical and Computational Semantics, pp. 43–53. Association for Computational Linguistics, New Orleans, Louisiana (Jun 2018). https://doi.org/10.18653/v1/S18-2005, https://www.aclweb.org/anthology/S18-2005
100. Kiritchenko, S., Mohammad, S.: Examining gender and race bias in two hundred sentiment analysis systems. In: Proceedings of the Seventh Joint Conference on Lexical and Computational Semantics, pp. 43–53. Association for Computational Linguistics, New Orleans, Louisiana (Jun 2018).https://doi.org/10.18653/v1/S18-2005, https://www.aclweb.org/anthology/S18-2005
101. Kłosok, M., Chlebus, M., et al.: Towards better understanding of complex machine learning models using explainable artificial intelligence (XAI): case of credit scoring modelling. University of Warsaw, Faculty of Economic Sciences Warsaw (2020)
102. Koh, P.W.W., Ang, K.S., Teo, H., Liang, P.S.: On the accuracy of influence functions for measuring group effects. Adv. Neural. Inf. Process. Syst. **32** (2019)
103. Kowalska, B., Kwaśnicka, H.: Unboxing the black box: mechanistic interpretability for algorithmic understanding of neural networks (2025). arXiv preprint arXiv:2511.19265
104. Krause, D., Krause, E.: Int. J. Artif. Intell. Mach. Learn. (2025)
105. Krizhevsky, A., Sutskever, I., Hinton, G.E.: Imagenet classification with deep convolutional neural networks. In: Advances in Neural Information Processing Systems, p. 25 (2012)
106. Kusner, M.J., Loftus, J., Russell, C., Silva, R.: Counterfactual fairness. Adv. Neural Inf. Process. Syst. **30** (2017)
107. Lakkaraju, K., Gupta, A., Srivastava, B., Valtorta, M., Wu, D.: The effect of human v/s synthetic test data and round-tripping on assessment of sentiment analysis systems for bias. In: 2023 5th IEEE International Conference on Trust, Privacy and Security in Intelligent Systems and Applications (TPS-ISA), pp. 380–389. IEEE Computer Society, Los Alamitos, CA, USA (Nov 2023). https://doi.org/10.1109/TPS-ISA58951.2023.00053, https://doi.ieeecomputersociety.org/10.1109/TPS-ISA58951.2023.00053
108. Lakkaraju, K.: Why is my system biased?: Rating of AI systems through a causal lens. In: Proceedings of the 2022 AAAI/ACM Conference on AI, Ethics, and Society, p. 902. AIES '22, Association for Computing Machinery, New York, NY, USA (2022). https://doi.org/10.1145/3514094.3539556
109. Lakkaraju, K., Jones, S.E., Vuruma, S.K.R., Pallagani, V., Muppasani, B.C., Srivastava, B.: Llms for financial advisement: a fairness and efficacy study in personal decision making. In: Proceedings of the Fourth ACM International Conference on AI in Finance, pp. 100–107 (2023)

110. Lakkaraju, K., Kaur, R., Zehtabi, P., Patra, S., Valluru, S.L., Zeng, Z., Srivastava, B., Valtorta, M.: On creating a causally grounded usable rating method for assessing the robustness of foundation models supporting time series (2025). arXiv preprint arXiv:2502.12226
111. Lakkaraju, K., Kaur, R., Zeng, Z., Zehtabi, P., Patra, S., Srivastava, B., Valtorta, M.: Rating multi-modal time-series forecasting models (mm-tsfm) for robustness through a causal lens (2024). arXiv preprint arXiv:2406.12908
112. Lakkaraju, K., Srivastava, B., Valtorta, M.: Rating sentiment analysis systems for bias through a causal lens. IEEE Trans. Technol. Soc. 1–1 (2024). https://doi.org/10.1109/TTS.2024.3375519
113. Lakkaraju, K., Valluru, S.L., Srivastava, B.: Holistic explainable AI (H-XAI): extending transparency beyond developers in AI-driven decision making. arXiv preprint arXiv:2508.05792 (2025)
114. Lakkaraju, K., Valluru, S.L., Srivastava, B., Valtorta, M.: Arc: A tool to rate AI models for robustness through a causal lens. In: IJCAI 2025 Workshop on User-Aligned Assessment of Adaptive AI Systems
115. LeCun, Y., Bengio, Y., Hinton, G.: Deep learning. Nature **521**(7553), 436–444 (2015)
116. LeCun, Y., Boser, B., Denker, J.S., Henderson, D., Howard, R.E., Hubbard, W., Jackel, L.D.: Backpropagation applied to handwritten zip code recognition. Neural Comput. **1**(4), 541–551 (1989)
117. LeCun, Y., Bottou, L., Bengio, Y., Haffner, P.: Gradient-based learning applied to document recognition. Proc. IEEE **86**(11), 2278–2324 (2002)
118. Lee, D.K.C., Guan, C., Yu, Y., Ding, Q.: A comprehensive review of generative AI in finance. FinTech **3**(3), 460–478 (2024)
119. Lee, N.T.: Recommendations for responsible use of AI in financial services. Testimony to the U.S. House Financial Services Subcommittee on Digital Assets, Financial Technology, and Artificial Intelligence (September 2025), https://www.brookings.edu/articles/recommendations-for-responsible-use-of-ai-in-financial-services/
120. Linardatos, P., Papastefanopoulos, V., Kotsiantis, S.: Explainable AI: a review of machine learning interpretability methods. Entropy **23**(1), 18 (2020)
121. Loria, S.: textblob documentation. Release 0.15 **2** (2018)
122. Loyola-Gonzalez, O.: Black-box vs. white-box: understanding their advantages and weaknesses from a practical point of view. IEEE Access **7**, 154096–154113 (2019)
123. Lu, X., Calabrese, R.: The cohort shapley value to measure fairness in financing small and medium enterprises in the UK. Financ. Res. Lett. **58**, 104542 (2023)
124. Lundberg, S., Lee, S.I.: A unified approach to interpreting model predictions (2017). https://arxiv.org/abs/1705.07874
125. van der Maaten, L., Hinton, G.: Visualizing data using t-SNE. J. Mach. Learn. Res. **9**(86), 2579–2605 (2008), http://jmlr.org/papers/v9/vandermaaten08a.html
126. Madsen, A., Chandar, S., Reddy, S.: Are self-explanations from large language models faithful? arXiv preprint arXiv:2401.07927 (2024)
127. Makhlouf, K., Zhioua, S., Palamidessi, C.: When causality meets fairness: a survey. J. Log. Algebr. Methods Program. **141**, 101000 (2024). https://doi.org/10.1016/j.jlamp.2024.101000, https://www.sciencedirect.com/science/article/pii/S2352220824000543
128. Makridakis, S., Spiliotis, E., Assimakopoulos, V.: M5 accuracy competition: results, findings, and conclusions. Int. J. Forecast. **38**(4), 1346–1364 (2022)
129. Malmqvist, L.: Sycophancy in large language models: causes and mitigations. In: Intelligent Computing-Proceedings of the Computing Conference, pp. 61–74. Springer (2025)
130. Mao, C., Xia, K., Wang, J., Wang, H., Yang, J., Bareinboim, E., Vondrick, C.: Causal transportability for visual recognition. In: Proceedings of the IEEE/CVF Conference on Computer Vision and Pattern Recognition, pp. 7521–7531 (2022)

131. Martins, T., De Almeida, A.M., Cardoso, E., Nunes, L.: Explainable artificial intelligence (XAI): a systematic literature review on taxonomies and applications in finance. IEEE Access **12**, 618–629 (2023)
132. McCarthy, J., Minsky, M.L., Rochester, N., Shannon, C.E.: A proposal for the dartmouth summer research project on artificial intelligence, August 31, 1955. AI Mag. **27**(4), 12–12 (2006)
133. McCulloch, W.S., Pitts, W.: A logical calculus of the ideas immanent in nervous activity. Bull. Math. Biophys. **5**(4), 115–133 (1943)
134. McInnes, L., Healy, J., Melville, J.: UMAP: uniform manifold approximation and projection for dimension reduction (2020). https://arxiv.org/abs/1802.03426
135. Meakin, H., Dulieu, R.: AI regulation in financial services: FCA developments and emerging enforcement risks. https://www.regulationtomorrow.com/eu/ai-regulation-in-financial-services-fca-developments-and-emerging-enforcement-risks/ (July 2025), regulation Tomorrow blog
136. Mehrotra, S., Huang, J., Fu, X., Dobbe, R., Sánchez, C.I., de Rijke, M.: Understanding AI trustworthiness: a scoping review of AIES & FAccT articles. arXiv preprint arXiv:2510.21293 (2025)
137. Melsom, B., Vennerød, C.B., de Lange, P.E.: Explainable artificial intelligence for credit scoring in banking. J. Risk (2022)
138. Mikolov, T., Sutskever, I., Chen, K., Corrado, G.S., Dean, J.: Distributed representations of words and phrases and their compositionality. Adv. Neural. Inf. Process. Syst. **26** (2013)
139. Miller, J., Hsu, C., Troutman, J., Perdomo, J., Zrnic, T., Liu, L., Sun, Y., Schmidt, L., Hardt, M.: Whynot (2020). https://doi.org/10.5281/zenodo.3875775
140. Miller, T.: Explainable AI is dead, long live explainable AI! hypothesis-driven decision support using evaluative AI. In: Proceedings of the 2023 ACM Conference on Fairness, Accountability, and Transparency, pp. 333–342 (2023)
141. Minsky, M., Papert, S.: An introduction to computational geometry. Cambridge Tiass., HIT **479**(480), 104 (1969)
142. Mishev, K., Gjorgjevikj, A., Vodenska, I., Chitkushev, L.T., Trajanov, D.: Evaluation of sentiment analysis in finance: from lexicons to transformers. IEEE Access **8**, 131662–131682 (2020). https://doi.org/10.1109/ACCESS.2020.3009626
143. Mnih, V., Kavukcuoglu, K., Silver, D., Rusu, A.A., Veness, J., Bellemare, M.G., Graves, A., Riedmiller, M., Fidjeland, A.K., Ostrovski, G.: Human-level control through deep reinforcement learning. Nature **518**(7540), 529–533 (2015)
144. Mohammad, S.M., Turney, P.D.: Crowdsourcing a word-emotion association lexicon. Comput. Intell. **29**(3), 436–465 (2013)
145. Morris, J., Lifland, E., Yoo, J.Y., Grigsby, J., Jin, D., Qi, Y.: Textattack: a framework for adversarial attacks, data augmentation, and adversarial training in NLP. In: Proceedings of the 2020 Conference on Empirical Methods in Natural Language Processing: System Demonstrations, pp. 119–126 (2020)
146. Mothilal, R.K., Sharma, A., Tan, C.: Explaining machine learning classifiers through diverse counterfactual explanations. In: Proceedings of the 2020 Conference on Fairness, Accountability, and Transparency, pp. 607–617 (2020)
147. Mueller, S.T., Hoffman, R.R., Clancey, W., Emrey, A., Klein, G.: Explanation in human-AI systems: a literature meta-review, synopsis of key ideas and publications, and bibliography for explainable AI (2019). arXiv preprint arXiv:1902.01876
148. Nabi, R., Shpitser, I.: Fair inference on outcomes. In: Proceedings of the AAAI Conference on Artificial Intelligence, vol. 32 (2018)
149. Nagpal, V., Valluru, S.L., Lakkaraju, K., Gupta, N., Abdulrahman, Z., Davison, A., Srivastava, B.: A novel approach to balance convenience and nutrition in meals with long-term group rec-

ommendations and reasoning on multimodal recipes and its implementation in beacon (2024). arXiv preprint arXiv:2412.17910
150. Nagpal, V., Valluru, S.L., Lakkaraju, K., Srivastava, B.: Beacon: balancing convenience and nutrition in meals with long-term group recommendations and reasoning on multimodal recipes (2024). arXiv preprint arXiv:2406.13714
151. Naimi, A.I., Cole, S.R., Kennedy, E.H.: An introduction to g methods. Int. J. Epidemiol. **46**(2), 756–762 (2017)
152. Nauta, M., Bucur, D., Seifert, C.: Causal discovery with attention-based convolutional neural networks. Mach. Learn. Knowl. Extr. **1**(1), 19 (2019)
153. Newell, A., Simon, H.: The logic theory machine-a complex information processing system. IRE Trans. Inf. Theory **2**(3), 61–79 (1956)
154. Neyman, J.: Sur les applications de la theorie des probabilites aux experiences agricoles: Essai des principes (in polish) in: Dabrowska dm, speed tp, translators. Stat. Sci. **5**, 465–480 (1923)
155. Nicolae, M.I., Sinn, M., Tran, M.N., Buesser, B., Rawat, A., Wistuba, M., Zantedeschi, V., Baracaldo, N., Chen, B., Ludwig, H.: Adversarial robustness toolbox v1. 0.0. arXiv preprint arXiv:1807.01069 (2018)
156. Nwachukwu, P., Chima, O., Okolo, C.: The artificial intelligence governance framework for finance: a control-by-design approach to algorithmic decision-making in accounting. Financ. Account. Res. J. **7**, 350–379 (2025). https://doi.org/10.51594/farj.v7i8.2016
157. Olko, M., Gajewski, M., Wojciechowska, J., Morzy, M., Sankowski, P.: Since faithfulness fails: the performance limits of neural causal discovery (2025). arXiv preprint arXiv:2502.16056
158. Olson, J.N.: What Might Have Been: The Social Psychology of Counterfactual Thinking, vol. 1. Giuseppe Castrovilli (1995)
159. Papernot, N., Faghri, F., Carlini, N., Goodfellow, I., Feinman, R., Kurakin, A., Xie, C., Sharma, Y., Brown, T., Roy, A.: Technical report on the cleverhans v2. 1.0 adversarial examples library (2016). arXiv preprint arXiv:1610.00768
160. Pearl, J.: Causality. Cambridge University Press (2009)
161. Pearl, J.: Causality. Cambridge University Press (2009)
162. Pearl, J.: Probabilistic Reasoning in Intelligent Systems: Networks of Plausible Inference. Elsevier (2014)
163. Pearl, J.: Fusion, propagation, and structuring in belief networks. In: Probabilistic and Causal Inference: The Works of Judea Pearl, pp. 139–188 (2022)
164. Pérez-Cruz, F., Prenio, J., Restoy, F., Yong, J.: Managing explanations: how regulators can address AI explainability. FSI Occasional Paper 24, Bank for International Settlements (September 2025), https://www.bis.org/fsi/fsipapers24.pdf
165. Phipps, M.E.: What's going on with our peanut butter nutrition labels? https://www.crazyrichards.com/whats-going-on-with-our-peanut-butter-nutrition-labels/, accessed: 2025-09-04
166. Plečko, D., Bareinboim, E.: Causal fairness analysis: A causal toolkit for fair machine learning. Found. Trends® Mach. Learn. **17**(3), 304–589 (2024)
167. Qiu, Z., Liu, W., Feng, H., Liu, Z., Xiao, T.Z., Collins, K.M., Tenenbaum, J.B., Weller, A., Black, M.J., Schölkopf, B.: Can large language models understand symbolic graphics programs? arXiv preprint arXiv:2408.08313 (2024)
168. Radford, A., Kim, J.W., Hallacy, C., Ramesh, A., Goh, G., Agarwal, S., Sastry, G., Askell, A., Mishkin, P., Clark, J., Krueger, G., Sutskever, I.: Learning transferable visual models from natural language supervision (2021)
169. Radford, A., Narasimhan, K., Salimans, T., Sutskever, I.: Improving language understanding by generative pre-training (2018)

170. Raffel, C., Shazeer, N., Roberts, A., Lee, K., Narang, S., Matena, M., Zhou, Y., Li, W., Liu, P.J.: Exploring the limits of transfer learning with a unified text-to-text transformer. J. Mach. Learn. Res. **21**(140), 1–67 (2020)
171. Ramsey, J., Zhang, J., Spirtes, P.L.: Adjacency-faithfulness and conservative causal inference (2012). arXiv preprint arXiv:1206.6843
172. Rando, J., Zhang, J., Carlini, N., Tramèr, F.: Adversarial ml problems are getting harder to solve and to evaluate (2025). arXiv preprint arXiv:2502.02260
173. Ribeiro, M.T., Singh, S., Guestrin, C.: "why should i trust you?" explaining the predictions of any classifier. In: Proceedings of the 22nd ACM SIGKDD International Conference on Knowledge Discovery and Data Mining, pp. 1135–1144 (2016)
174. Ribeiro, M.T., Wu, T., Guestrin, C., Singh, S.: Beyond accuracy: behavioral testing of NLP models with checklist (2020). arXiv preprint arXiv:2005.04118
175. Richardson, B., Gilbert, J.E.: A framework for fairness: a systematic review of existing fair AI solutions (2021). arXiv preprint arXiv:2112.05700
176. Rios, F.L., Moffa, G., Kuipers, J.: Benchpress: a scalable and platform-independent workflow for benchmarking structure learning algorithms for graphical models. arXiv preprint arXiv (2021)
177. Rosenbaum, P.R.: Sensitivity analysis for certain permutation inferences in matched observational studies. Biometrika **74**(1), 13–26 (1987)
178. Rosenbaum, P.R., Rubin, D.B.: The central role of the propensity score in observational studies for causal effects. Biometrika **70**(1), 41–55 (1983)
179. Rosenblatt, F.: The perceptron: a probabilistic model for information storage and organization in the brain. Psychol. Rev. **65**(6), 386 (1958)
180. Rothman, K.J., Greenland, S.: Causation and causal inference in epidemiology. Am. J. Public Health **95**(S1), S144–S150 (2005)
181. Rubin, D.B.: Estimating causal effects of treatments in randomized and nonrandomized studies. J. Educ. Psychol. **66**(5), 688 (1974)
182. Rudin, C.: Stop explaining black box machine learning models for high stakes decisions and use interpretable models instead. Nat. Mach. Intell. **1**(5), 206–215 (2019)
183. Rumelhart, D.E., Hinton, G.E., Williams, R.J.: Learning representations by back-propagating errors. Nature **323**(6088), 533–536 (1986)
184. Russell, S.J., Norvig, P.: Artificial Intelligence: A Modern Approach. Pearson (2016)
185. Scipy: Morlet 2 - scipy.signal.morlet2. https://docs.scipy.org/doc/scipy-1.11.3/reference/generated/scipy.signal.morlet2.html (2024), accessed: 2024-05-13
186. Selvaraju, R.R., Cogswell, M., Das, A., Vedantam, R., Parikh, D., Batra, D.: Grad-cam: visual explanations from deep networks via gradient-based localization. In: Proceedings of the IEEE International Conference on Computer Vision, pp. 618–626 (2017)
187. Shamsabadi, A.S., Wyllie, S.C., Franzese, N., Dullerud, N., Gambs, S., Papernot, N., Wang, X., Weller, A.: Confidential-profitt: confidential proof of fair training of trees. In: The Eleventh International Conference on Learning Representations (2022)
188. Shannon, C.E.: A mathematical theory of communication. Bell Syst. Tech. J. **27**(3), 379–423 (1948)
189. Sharma, A., Kiciman, E.: Dowhy: an end-to-end library for causal inference (2020). arXiv preprint arXiv:2011.04216
190. Sharma, M., Tong, M., Korbak, T., Duvenaud, D., Askell, A., Bowman, S.R., Cheng, N., Durmus, E., Hatfield-Dodds, Z., Johnston, S.R.: Towards understanding sycophancy in language models (2023). arXiv preprint arXiv:2310.13548
191. Shortliffe, E.: Computer-Based Medical Consultations: MYCIN, vol. 2. Elsevier (2012)
192. Silva, R.: Counterfactual fairness is not demographic parity, and other observations (2024). arXiv preprint arXiv:2402.02663

193. Simonyan, K., Vedaldi, A., Zisserman, A.: Deep inside convolutional networks: visualising image classification models and saliency maps (2013). arXiv preprint arXiv:1312.6034
194. Simson, J., Fabris, A., Fröhner, C., Kreuter, F., Kern, C.: Bias begins with data: the fairground corpus for robust and reproducible research on algorithmic fairness (2025). arXiv preprint arXiv:2510.22363
195. Spirtes, P.: An anytime algorithm for causal inference. International Workshop on Artificial Intelligence and Statistics, pp. 278–285. PMLR (2001)
196. Spirtes, P., Glymour, C.N., Scheines, R.: Causation, Prediction, and Search. MIT Press (2000)
197. Spitzer, P., Holstein, J., Morrison, K., Holstein, K., Satzger, G., Kühl, N.: Don't be fooled: the misinformation effect of explanations in human–AI collaboration. Int. J. Hum.– Comput. Interact. 1–29 (2025)
198. Srivastava, B., Koppel, T., Paladi, S.T., Valluru, S.L., Sharma, R., Bond, O.: Ultra: a data-driven approach for recommending team formation in response to proposal calls. In: 2022 IEEE International Conference on Data Mining Workshops (ICDMW), pp. 1002–1009. IEEE (2022)
199. Srivastava, B., Lakkaraju, K., Bernagozzi, M., Valtorta, M.: Advances in automatically rating the trustworthiness of text processing services (2023)
200. Srivastava, B., Rossi, F.: Towards composable bias rating of AI services. In: Proceedings of the 2018 AAAI/ACM Conference on AI, Ethics, and Society, pp. 284–289 (2018)
201. Srivastava, B., Rossi, F.: Towards composable bias rating of AI systems. In: 2018 AI Ethics and Society Conference (AIES 2018), New Orleans, Louisiana, USA, Feb 2-3 (2018)
202. Srivastava, B., Rossi, F.: Rating AI systems for bias to promote trustable applications. IBM J. Res. Dev. (2020)
203. Srivastava, B., Rossi, F., Usmani, S., Bernagozzi, M.: Personalized chatbot trustworthiness ratings. IEEE Trans. Technol. Soc. (2020)
204. Srivastava, B., Rossi, F., Usmani, S., Bernagozzi, M.: Personalized chatbot trustworthiness ratings. IEEE Trans. Technol. Soc. **1**(4), 184–192 (2020). https://doi.org/10.1109/TTS.2020.3023919
205. Stanton, J.M.: Galton, pearson, and the peas: a brief history of linear regression for statistics instructors. J. Stat. Educ. **9**(3) (2001)
206. Stuart, E.A.: Propensity scores and matching methods. In: The Reviewer's Guide to Quantitative Methods in the Social Sciences, pp. 388–396. Routledge (2018)
207. Su, J., Vargas, D.V., Sakurai, K.: One pixel attack for fooling deep neural networks. IEEE Trans. Evol. Comput. **23**(5), 828–841 (2019)
208. Sudjianto, A., Knauth, W., Singh, R., Yang, Z., Zhang, A.: Unwrapping the black box of deep relu networks: interpretability, diagnostics, and simplification (2020). arXiv:2011.04041
209. Sudjianto, A., Zhang, A., Yang, Z., Su, Y., Zeng, N.: Piml toolbox for interpretable machine learning model development and diagnostics (2023)
210. Sundararajan, M., Taly, A., Yan, Q.: Axiomatic attribution for deep networks. In: International Conference on Machine Learning, pp. 3319–3328. PMLR (2017)
211. Sutton, R.S.: Learning to predict by the methods of temporal differences. Mach. Learn. **3**(1), 9–44 (1988)
212. Tao, Z., Zhang, J., Li, H., Li, X., Peng, Y., Liu, X., Wang, S., Liu, C., Ren, S., Zhang, S.: Humanoid-inspired causal representation learning for domain generalization. arXiv preprint arXiv:2510.16382 (2025)
213. Team, G.: Gemini: a family of highly capable multimodal models (2024), https://arxiv.org/abs/2312.11805
214. Tian, X., Nunes, B.P., Grant, K., Casanova, M.A.: Mitigating bias in glam search engines: a simple rating-based approach and reflection. In: Proceedings of the 34th ACM Conference on Hypertext and Social Media. HT '23, Association for Computing Machinery, New York, NY, USA (2023).https://doi.org/10.1145/3603163.3609043

215. Tilouche, S., Partovi Nia, V., Bassetto, S.: Parallel coordinate order for high-dimensional data. Stat. Anal. Data Min. **14**(5), 501–515 (2021)
216. Turing, A.: Computing machinery and intelligence. Mind **59**(236), 433–60 (1950). https://doi.org/10.1093/mind/lix.236.433
217. Turing, A.M., et al.: On computable numbers, with an application to the entscheidungsproblem. J. Math. **58**(345–363), 5 (1936)
218. Upadhyaya, P., Zhang, K., Li, C., Jiang, X., Kim, Y., et al.: Scalable causal structure learning: scoping review of traditional and deep learning algorithms and new opportunities in biomedicine. JMIR Med. Inform. **11**(1), e38266 (2023)
219. Valluru, S.L., Srivastava, B., Paladi, S.T., Yan, S., Natarajan, S.: Promoting research collaboration with open data driven team recommendation in response to call for proposals. In: Proceedings of the AAAI Conference on Artificial Intelligence, vol. 38, pp. 22833–22841 (2024)
220. Valluru, S.L., Widener, M., Srivastava, B., Gangopadhyay, S.: Ultra: Exploring team recommendations in two geographies using open data in response to call for proposals. In: Proceedings of the 7th Joint International Conference on Data Science & Management of Data (11th ACM IKDD CODS and 29th COMAD). pp. 547–552 (2024)
221. Valluru, S.L., Widener, M., Srivastava, B., Natarajan, S., Gangopadhyay, S.: Ai-assisted research collaboration with open data for fair and effective response to call for proposals. AI Mag. **45**(4), 457–471 (2024)
222. Vapnik, V.: Support-vector networks. Mach. Learn. **20**, 273–297 (1995)
223. Vaswani, A., Shazeer, N., Parmar, N., Uszkoreit, J., Jones, L., Gomez, A.N., Kaiser, Ł., Polosukhin, I.: Attention is all you need. Adv. Neural Inf. Process. Syst. **30** (2017)
224. Verma, S., Rubin, J.: Fairness definitions explained. In: Proceedings of the International Workshop on Software Fairness, pp. 1–7 (2018)
225. Wachter, S., Mittelstadt, B., Russell, C.: Counterfactual explanations without opening the black box: automated decisions and the GDPR. Harv. JL & Tech. **31**, 841 (2017)
226. Wang, Z.: Causalbench: a comprehensive benchmark for evaluating causal reasoning capabilities of large language models. In: Proceedings of the 10th SIGHAN Workshop on Chinese Language Processing (SIGHAN-10), pp. 143–151 (2024)
227. Weber, P., Carl, K.V., Hinz, O.: Applications of explainable artificial intelligence in finance-a systematic review of finance, information systems, and computer science literature. Manag. Rev. Q. **74**(2), 867–907 (2024)
228. Wei, J., Wang, X., Schuurmans, D., Bosma, M., Xia, F., Chi, E., Le, Q.V., Zhou, D., et al.: Chain-of-thought prompting elicits reasoning in large language models. Adv. Neural. Inf. Process. Syst. **35**, 24824–24837 (2022)
229. Widener, M., Lakkaraju, K., Aydin, J., Srivastava, B.: On identifying why and when foundation models perform well on time-series forecasting using automated explanations and rating (2025). arXiv preprint arXiv:2508.20437
230. Wu, S., Irsoy, O., Lu, S., Dabravolski, V., Dredze, M., Gehrmann, S., Kambadur, P., Rosenberg, D., Mann, G.: Bloomberggpt: a large language model for finance (2023). arXiv preprint arXiv:2303.17564
231. Xia, K., Lee, K.Z., Bengio, Y., Bareinboim, E.: The causal-neural connection: expressiveness, learnability, and inference. Adv. Neural. Inf. Process. Syst. **34**, 10823–10836 (2021)
232. Yanglet, X.Y.L., Cao, Y., Deng, L.: Multimodal financial foundation models (mffms. In: Progress, Prospects, and Challenges (2025). arXiv preprint arXiv:2506.01973
233. Zemel, R., Wu, Y., Swersky, K., Pitassi, T., Dwork, C.: Learning fair representations. In: International Conference on Machine Learning, pp. 325–333. PMLR (2013)
234. Zeng, Z., Kaur, R., Siddagangappa, S., Balch, T., Veloso, M.: From pixels to predictions: Spectrogram and vision transformer for better time series forecasting. In: Proceedings of the

Fourth ACM International Conference on AI in Finance, pp. 82–90. ICAIF '23, Association for Computing Machinery, New York, NY, USA (2023). https://doi.org/10.1145/3604237.3626905

235. Zhang, K., Zhu, S., Kalander, M., Ng, I., Ye, J., Chen, Z., Pan, L.: gcastle: a python toolbox for causal discovery (2021). arXiv preprint arXiv:2111.15155
236. Zhang, L., Wu, Y., Wu, X.: A causal framework for discovering and removing direct and indirect discrimination (2016). arXiv preprint arXiv:1611.07509
237. Zhang, M., Fu, J., Warrier, T., Wang, Y., Tan, T., Huang, K.W.: Faith: a framework for assessing intrinsic tabular hallucinations in finance. In: Proceedings of the 6th ACM International Conference on AI in Finance, pp. 159–167 (2025)
238. Zhu, T., Yin, Z., Lyu, W., Zhang, J., Luo, B.: Imperceptible adversarial attack on S channel of HSV colorspace. In: 2023 International Joint Conference on Neural Networks (IJCNN), pp. 1–7 (2023). https://doi.org/10.1109/IJCNN54540.2023.10191049
239. Zilke, J.R., Loza Mencía, E., Janssen, F.: Deepred–rule extraction from deep neural networks. In: International Conference on Discovery Science, pp. 457–473. Springer (2016)

Index

K. Lakkaraju and B. Srivastava, *Assessing, Explaining, and Rating AI Systems for Trust*, Synthesis Lectures on Computer Science, https://doi.org/10.1007/978-3-032-21039-5

The manufacturer's authorised representative in the EU is Springer Nature Customer Service Centre GmbH, Europaplatz 3, 69115 Heidelberg, Germany. If you have any concerns regarding our products, please contact ProductSafety@springernature.com

Printed and bound by CPI Group (UK) Ltd, Croydon, CR0 4YY
10/08/2026
02192385-0004